ABERDEEN

OFFICIAL

ALL-TIME GREATS

Dave Macdermid

Lomond Books

A Grange Publication

© 1999

g Published by Grange Communications Ltd., Edinburgh, under licence from Aberdeen Football Club.

Printed in the EU.

Photographs supplied by D. C. Thomson & Co. Ltd.

ISBN: 1-84204-004-9

CONTENTS

INTRODUCTION

Being asked to write a brief summary on fifty 'Aberdeen All-time Greats and Legends' is easier said than done. After all, football is completely subjective and we all have our own ideas as to who would comprise the top fifty and who would not.

Also, on what criteria do you decide who to include? Is it the most skilful? The most popular with the fans? The most loyal? The parameters are endless.

In the end, it came down to a number of diverse reasons. Not necessarily the most talented, not always the most obvious but players who have all made a major contribution to the history of Aberdeen Football Club in one way or another.

It is also simply a fact of human nature that you tend to remember with most fondness, the players from the era during which you spent your formative years. Consequently, I make no apology for the imbalance which is geared towards the sixties and seventies within these pages.

Also included are all of the starting line-up from that marvellous wet evening in Gothenburg on 11th May 1983, plus John Hewitt of course, when Aberdeen lifted the European Cup Winners' Cup in such dramatic fashion. When Teddy Scott was asked to name the greatest ever Dons team, that was the eleven he selected and quite rightly, too.

It is also, perhaps, indicative of Aberdeen's recent fortunes, that only Jim Leighton and Eoin Jess of the squad currently employed at Pittodrie find their way into the fifty, along with Duncan Shearer and Brian Irvine from the not-too-distant past.

CONTINUED OVER . . .

The truth of the matter is that it would be very easy to name a second fifty players, most of whom are as well known, skilful, etc as many of those included. Billy Dodds, Hans Gillhaus, Charlie Nicholas Steve Murray, Eddie Falloon and Alex Jackson would all be definite inclusions in many fans' top fifty and indeed, other than Willie Miller, Alex McLeish, Jim Leighton, Joe Harper and Zoltan Varga......... oops, there I go again, making the assumption that the aforementioned would be in every Dons fans top players list.

This is not a book for the football anorak, more just a passing glimpse into the highlights of fifty men who have graced the red, or in some cases black and gold, shirt of Aberdeen Football Club. Apologies to all those players and former stars who have been omitted and if you don't believe me when I say it was an extremely difficult task to whittle things down to fifty names, try it yourself!

Dave Macdermid.

ZOLTAN VARGA

oltan's stay with Aberdeen Football Club lasted less than a year but he is regarded by many Dons fans to be the most skilful player ever to grace Pittodrie Stadium.

A Hungarian International, he joined the Dons from Hertha Berlin in October 1972, where he had been banned by the German authorities for his part in a bribery scandal in Germany, and made his debut against Falkirk on 14th October 1972 in a 2-2 draw.

As Jack Webster said in his excellent book The Dons – The History of Aberdeen Football Club "If football were a wine, then here was the vintage champagne, a heady experience which was surely too good to last."

Although his time at Pittodrie was all too brief, Zoltan produced many memories for the Dons support, some of which are well worth looking back on again.

His first goal for the Pittodrie team was in a memorable match, to say the least. The Dons were at home to league leaders Celtic on the 28th October, and found themselves two goals down after only sixteen minutes. That inspired a Zoltan led fightback. His first goal was a swerving 20 yard strike, his second effort, a lob over visiting keeper Evan Williams. Celtic still won 3-2 but Zoltan had made his mark at Pittodrie.

Another double for the Hungarian came against Morton at Pittodrie on 23rd December. Again, he demonstrated his belief that variety is the spice of life with his first goal an unstoppable 30 yarder and his second, a deft header. By now, Zoltan was regarded very much as a hero by the Red Army, who are turning out in force just to see him play.

By this time, back in Germany, his previous club, Hertha Berlin, had had a change of heart and wanted their star player back. Hearing the news, the Hungarian maestro asked for a transfer and in the summer of 1973, to the great disappointment of Aberdeen fans everywhere, he was back in Germany, although not for long.

Johan Cryuff had joined Barcelona for £1,000,000 and Ajax desperately needed to replace the influential midfielder. Who else, but the enigmatic Hungarian who, just as he had done at Pittodrie, became an instant hero with the Amsterdam faithful. Upon retiring, Zoltan took up a coaching position in West Germany and managed Croatia Zagreb in 1998 when they faced Newcastle in the Champions League qualifier.

Six months of incredible passing and finishing, and all round sublime skills had been witnessed at Pittodrie. That was all that was needed to convince many they had seen one of the true great players to play for the Dons.

STEWART McKIMMIE

Picking up a European Super Cup winner's medal less than a month after joining a club is no mean achievement and that's exactly what happened to Stewart following his transfer from Dundee in December 1993.

The Aberdeen born full-back had gone to Dens three years previously from Banks O'Dee and he made his Aberdeen debut in a 2-1 home win over Hibs on 17th December 1983, just three days prior to the second leg of the Super Cup match with Hamburg.

By the end of that season, Stewart had added League Championship and Scottish Cup winners medals to his collection and a Dons career which was to last fourteen years was well on its way.

In his early years at Pittodrie, Stewart became well used to picking up honours with another league title, the Scottish Cup and the Skol Cup won over a period of two seasons.

However, if Stewart thought this was going to be the norm throughout his career, he was substantially off the mark and there then followed a fairly lean time of things.

The Skol Cup final of 1987-88 was snatched by Rangers on penalty kicks and twelve months later the Ibrox side retained the trophy, this time winning 3-2 inside ninety minutes.

Things looked up again in 1989-90, the double cup winning season, when Rangers and then Celtic were dispatched and, on a personal level, it was around this time Stewart had started to be recognised on the international scene, where he was to eventually pick up forty caps.

The next opportunity for honours came in 1992-3 and although injury ruled Stewart out of the Skol Cup Final on 25th October 1992, won 2-1 by Rangers, he was at right back as normal for the final of the Scottish Cup, against the same opposition, on 29th May 1993. Sadly, the outcome was the same too, 2-1 to Rangers.

At the start of the 1994-5 term, Stewart was made team captain, replacing the now departed Alex McLeish. It turned out to be a season memorable for all the wrong reasons including losses to Skonto Riga in the UEFA Cup and Stenhousemuir in the Tennents Scottish Cup, plus escaping relegation by the skin of the club's teeth via the newly introduced play-off system.

Demonstrating just how fickle the game of football is, a mere six months later Stewart was at Hampden lifting the now renamed Coca-Cola Cup after a 2-0 final win over Dundee. And after coming so close to going down the previous season, in the league Aberdeen finished a very creditable third.

Towards the end of the following season, Stewart was informed by manager Roy Aitken that his services were no longer required and he was quickly snapped up by rivals Dundee United, where he spent a further season before hanging up his boots. Stewart is now heavily involved in the media as a television and radio pundit as well as a contributor for the Aberdeen Evening Express.

NEALE COOPER

product of the Aberdeen youth system, Neale, who joined the Pittodrie playing staff straight from school, was originally a sweeper. However, the form of one Willie Miller ensured that progress in that particular direction was not a viable option.

Instead, Neale found his niche in midfield where he quickly earned a reputation as a determined ball-winner. That aside, he did make his debut, aged sixteen, at centre-half, in a 2-0 Pittodrie win against Kilmarnock on 11th October 1980.

The fact that Neale was a member of the team that produced the greatest result in the history of Aberdeen Football Club ensures his place in the hearts of Dons fans for time immemorial. In his six seasons with Aberdeen's first team, he scored ten times in two hundred and forty-five appearances, twenty-five of which were as a substitute.

Of those ten goals, the one most remembered by Dons fans is undoubtedly the extra time thump into the net from a distance of about six inches which completed the 4-1 humiliation of Rangers in the Scottish Cup Final of 1982.

And it was in a Cup Final, the 3-0 win over Hearts in 1986, that Neale played his last game for Aberdeen, prior to moving south with Aston Villa and then returning to Scotland with Rangers.

A career which included spells at Reading, Dunfermline Athletic and then Ross County followed, with the Dingwall club giving Neale the opportunity to cut his teeth in management when Bobby Wilson left Victoria Park.

Alex Ferguson has admitted that he probably played some of his younger players too often in the early eighties, resulting in their being 'burnt out' way before their time. Certainly, Neale was one of those being referred to, as he most definitely did not realise fully the potential he undoubtedly possessed.

What he missed out on, though, as a player, he does not look like repeating as a manager. At time of writing, after missing out twelve months previously by the narrowest of margins, he has just gained promotion to the Scottish Second Division and demonstrated real ambition by beating off the challenges of several clubs in higher divisions to land the signature of another ex-Don, Brian Irvine.

With the help of a very strong Pittodrie connection in Dingwall, including Nicky Walker and Kenny Gilbert, there is every possibility that Ross County could be a First Division or even Premier League club within the next three or four seasons. If that does, indeed, happen, then much of the credit will be down to the man who wore the number 4 shirt on that wet night in Gothenburg on the 11th May 1983.

JIM BETT

The silky Hamilton-born midfielder's career is testament to the adage that football is, indeed, a funny old game! Signed on an 'S' form by Dundee, then allowed to move to Airdrie and then Valur of Iceland, Jim looked destined to be given that perennial tag, 'journeyman player'.

However, a move to Belgian side, FC Lokeren, in 1979 proved to be the catalyst for a significant upturn in Jim's fortunes and within a year he had attracted the attentions of Rangers, to whom he was transferred for a fee of £180,000 in June 1980.

Jim spent three seasons at Ibrox, during which time his displays rightly earned him a Scotland call-up, winning the first of his twenty-five international caps against Holland in 1982.

In May of the following year, Jim returned to Lokeren, where he spent a further two years before being snapped up by the Dons in the close season of 1985, for a fee of £300,000.

Jim marked his Dons debut with the opener in a 3-0 Pittodrie win over Hibs and although the early months of his Pittodrie career were hampered by a variety of injuries, his artistry and vision in the middle of the park quickly established him as a favourite in the eyes of the Red Army.

That first season was marked by the lifting of the Scottish Cup, with Jim playing a prominent role in the 3-0 final success over Hearts. Over the next few seasons, he was a top team regular and in 1990-91, when the Dons pushed Rangers right to the infamous last day at Ibrox for the league title, he was the only Aberdeen player to feature in all league matches.

Jim continued at Pittodrie until season 1993-94, by which time his appearances in the first team had been restricted through injury and the arrival of younger team-mates, such as Paul Kane and Lee Richardson. Following his departure from Pittodrie, Jim was quickly snapped up by Hearts, where he was virtually an ever-present in season 1994-95. He then spent a year at Tannadice, helping Dundee United out of the First Division before retiring from playing.

The Bett connection still lives on at Aberdeen Football Club through sons, Baldur and Calum, both of whom are tipped to follow their father right to the top. Whilst they may well end up being internationals, it will not be in the blue of Scotland, as both have opted to play for Iceland, the home country of their mother.

STEVE ARCHIBALD

Signed from Clyde at the beginning of 1978 by Billy McNeill, Steve Archibald made his Aberdeen debut in the somewhat inauspicious surroundings of Somerset Park, playing his part in a 1-1 draw. The Red Army did not take long to warm to the blond striker – a double at Ibrox, helping Aberdeen to a 3-0 win in March, saw to that!

From the outset, Archibald struck up what was to prove quite a fruitful partnership with Joe Harper and in his first full season, 1978-79, the pair of them contributed fifty-three goals between them.

Season 1979-80 began with a disappointing single-goal defeat at the hands of Partick Thistle and ended with the league title being won with a 5-0 Easter Road thumping of Hibs, in which Archibald notched the opener. He finished as Dons' top scorer that season, with a haul of twenty-two goals, twelve of which were in the league.

Steve's scoring exploits had come to the attention of other clubs by this time and in May 1980 he was transferred to Spurs for a fee of £800,000. He was a revelation in his inaugural season in England, finishing as leading marksman in the old First Division, as well as picking up a coveted FA Cup winner's medal.

After four successful seasons south of the border, Steve was on the move again, this time trying his luck in Spain, with Barcelona, after moving for a fee of £1,150,000. There, as had been the case throughout his career, he enjoyed a fantastic opening spell with the Spanish giants, helping them to their first Spanish league title in eleven years.

A period of mediocre form saw Steve disappear from the limelight but after a spell out of the first team, he returned, ironically displacing another import, in the shape of Mark Hughes.

In 1988, Steve returned to Scotland with Hibs and on Guy Fawkes Day of that year, he opened the scoring in the first minute against the Dons. Fortunately, a Charlie Nicholas brace turned the game round the way of the Pittodrie side.

Following his stint at Easter Road, Steve enjoyed spells at St. Mirren and then back at his first club, Clyde, before moving to East Fife, where he became player-coach. A fallout with the powers that be at Bayview saw him resign and he is now on the staff at Portuguese giants, Benfica.

ALEX McLEISH

Signed from Glasgow United in 1976, Alex was eighteen when he played for the Dons' top team for the first time, in a 1-0 win over Dundee United on 2nd January 1978. That was his only appearance until the following season and in his early time with the Pittodrie club, Alex often lined-up in midfield, before settling at centre-half for the vast majority of a long and distinguished career.

The year of 1980 was a particularly memorable one for the tall Glaswegian. The Dons won the league championship and Alex won the first of his seventy-seven international caps. There then followed that halcyon period in which Aberdeen Football Club could do nothing wrong, winning honour upon honour.

Much of that success is down to the partnership of Alex and Willie Miller in the heart of the Dons rearguard, which, along with keeper, Jim Leighton, ensured Aberdeen had a defence ranked as one of the most miserly in Europe.

As with anyone who was in the side, Alex's best moment as a Don came in Gothenburg and he, more than most, had reason to be grateful to John Hewitt for his winner, as it had been his short pass back that culminated in opponents, Real Madrid's, leveller from the spot.

For most of his senior career with Aberdeen, Alex was used to deputising as team captain if Willie Miller was unfit and when injury forced Willie to retire at the beginning of the 1990-91 season, there was never any doubt as to who would be taking on the mantle.

Unfortunately, the taking over of the skipper's armband coincided with a fairly barren period in the Pittodrie club's history and for many, the shock loss of the league title to Rangers on the last Saturday of that first season, was the catalyst for much grief in the ensuing seasons.

On the eve of the following season, Alex sustained a chipped bone in his ankle, an injury which was to cause him to miss the bulk of that particular campaign, in which he made only seven appearances. And he certainly was missed, as the Dons never came close to having a sniff of success, with a poor league display and early cup exits, both domestically and in Europe.

A hamstring problem meant Alex was again missing at the start of the 1992-93 campaign and he missed Skol Cup Final defeat at the hands of Rangers on 25th October 1992. He was back in time for the start of the Tennents Scottish Cup run, which went all the way, only to be thwarted at the final hurdle by, who else but yet again, Rangers.

Alex stayed at Pittodrie until the summer of 1994 when, to the surprise of many, he was allowed to go to Motherwell as player-manager. He stayed at Fir Park until season 1997-98, becoming boss at Hibs, where he remains and at time of writing is looking forward to a return to the Scottish Premier League.

TOMMY CRAIG

lasgow-born Tommy was another to be discovered by the legendary Bobby Calder and he signed in 1966, after being spotted playing for Drumchapel Amateurs. At one point, it looked a certainty that the talented left-footer would be signing for Celtic but Bobby kept chipping away and eventually got his man.

The flame-haired midfielder made his debut on 16th December 1967 in a single goal win at home to Stirling Albion and on 10th February the following year, he celebrated his first senior goal, the opener in a 2-0 success at home to Hearts.

Tommy's stay at Pittodrie turned out to be an all-too-brief one. He played for most of the following season, still only a teenager, before becoming the first Scottish player to be transferred to an English club, in the shape of Sheffield Wednesday, for a six figure fee. He bade his farewells to the Red Army in a disappointing 1-0 home defeat at the hands of Kilmarnock on 19th April 1969.

He spent five years at Hillsborough and was then transferred to Newcastle United at the tail end of 1974. During his time at St James' Park, he was awarded his one and only Scotland cap, appearing against Switzerland in 1976.

Further moves followed in 1978 to Aston Villa and then to Swansea City the following year. After three years in Wales, Tommy found himself at Carlisle United where he enjoyed his first taste of football management.

John Blackley, the then boss at Hibs, persuaded him to return to Scotland as his assistant in 1984 and three years later he took up a similar post with Celtic, the club he had almost signed for as a youngster. His career then went full circle when, at the conclusion of the 1994-95 season, manager Roy Aitken brought him to Pittodrie as his assistant.

Following his dismissal, along with Roy, in November 1997, Tommy went back down south and is now at another of his former clubs, Newcastle United, where he looks after the youth teams.

BRIAN IRVINE

**S**igned by Alex Ferguson in 1985 from Falkirk, Brian would be the first to admit there are more skilful players in the world. Although that is certainly true, it is doubtful whether there are any braver.

Brian made his first-team debut in the final league game of 1985-86 and he could not have wished for an easier one, with the Dons winning 6-0 at bottom of the table Clydebank on 3rd May 1986.

In each of the following two seasons, Brian only played in around half of the matches. Hardly surprising, given that Alex McLeish and Willie Miller were both still an integral part of the set-up at that time.

The 1988-89 campaign saw Brian more involved on a regular basis and he was in the first team on thirty-five occasions. It was also a season of 'so near and yet so far', with second place in the league and a second successive Skol Cup Final defeat at the hands of Rangers.

Brian lifted his first silverware as a Don the following year, coming on as a substitute in the Skol Cup Final on 22nd October 1989, as Aberdeen at last gained revenge over Rangers, winning 2-1 after extra time. Then on 12th May 1990, in the Scottish Cup Final against Celtic, scoreless after a hundred and twenty minutes' play, the destination of the trophy was down to the outcome of a penalty shoot-out. With the scores tied at 8-8 and Anton Rogan's effort having been saved by Theo Snelders, Brian blasted the ball past Pat Bonner to win the Cup for the Dons.

Brian was very much part of the Dons set-up through the first part of the nineties. In season 1992-93 and again the following year, he played more league games than any other Aberdeen player, featuring in thirty-nine and then forty-two of the forty-four matches.

Brian continued to give excellent service to the Dons until his world almost literally fell apart in June 1995, when he was informed that he was suffering from the debilitating disease, multiple sclerosis. Many would have given in to such devastating news but not Brian and he battled back to fitness, returning in a friendly at Ross County.

Less than two years later, Brian received another blow when was told by manager, Roy Aitken, that he was being allowed to leave the club he loved, joining First Division, Dundee, on a free transfer and helping the Dens Parkers return to the Premier Division.

In the close season of 1998-89, Brian rejected a new contract from Dundee and teamed up at Ross County with former Don, Neale Cooper, signing a three-year deal with the ambitious Victoria Park side.

DREW JARVIE

L anarkshire born, Drew, first came to prominence with Airdrie, who he joined from juniors Kilsyth Rangers, forming an excellent partnership up front with another Drew, namely Busby.

Aberdeen paid £76,000 for his services in the summer of 1972 and he made a scoring debut on 12th August that year in a 4-0 League Cup success at Queen of the South. Indeed, Drew's Pittodrie career got off to a flying start and he scored in each of his first quartet of matches, six goals in total.

Drew finished his first season as the Dons' top scorer, with a tally of twenty-eight goals and for the next two seasons, he repeated the feat, this time with twenty-four and then thirteen goals.

The following season, the first of the newly created Premier League, was not a good one, either for Aberdeen Football Club or for Drew on a personal level. The team beat the drop by the skin of its teeth, finishing on the same points mark as relegated Dundee and Drew's goal supply dried up somewhat, with a mere five in forty appearances.

The return of former striking partner, Joe Harper, in time for the start of the 1976-77 campaign was a welcome boost for Drew, as the pair had combined well together prior to Joe's move to Everton.

It was Joe's head flick to Drew that allowed the latter to head home the equaliser in the League Cup Final victory over Celtic on 6th November 1976. The 2-1 success gave Drew his first taste of lifting silverware at Pittodrie, with the final whistle signalling scenes of unbridled joy in the Aberdeen camp.

The Jarvie-Harper strike force continued to wreak havoc in opposition defences over the next few seasons, although Joe missed much of the title-winning 1979-80 season due to injury. Drew played an important part in that campaign, with fourteen goals.

In the early eighties, with his best playing years now behind him, Drew's first-team outings were limited, although he was doing an excellent job, assisting some of the Pittodrie youngsters with their development in the reserves. His final game for the Dons was on 24th April 1982, when he came on as a substitute for Mark McGhee in a 2-0 Pittodrie victory over Airdrie.

In October 1983, Drew returned to Airdrie, after which he joined the management team at St Mirren, then Dundee, before coming back to the North East where, for the last few years, he has been responsible for youth development at Pittodrie.

WILLIE MILLER

As with Joe Harper, Willie is one Aberdeen player who would be among the first names included in any Dons fan's team of all time. And yet, when he first arrived in the NorthEast, in June 1971, he was signed as a striker, having been spotted playing for Glasgow side, Eastercraigs.

Willie was farmed out to Peterhead in his first season and continued to find the net regularly before being recalled by Aberdeen. He made his Dons debut in the last league game of 1972-73, coming on for Arthur Graham in the 2-1 Cappielow win on 28th April 1973.

By this time, with the aid of Dons great, Teddy Scott, Willie had been converted to a sweeper and from the beginning of season 1973-74, he became a first-team regular. The career of a true Aberdeen great was now well underway!

As Willie's reputation of being one of the best 'penalty box defenders' in the world grew, so, too, did the honours. Appointed Dons' club captain in December 1975, Willie was selected for Scotland in season 1975-76. That game, against Romania, signalled the first of no fewer than sixty-five caps won by the Glasgow-born defender.

His first domestic trophy was won with the lifting of the League Cup on 6th November 1976, in a 2-1 Hampden victory against Celtic. From that point on, for the next fourteen years or so, Willie was to pick up just about every honour up for grabs.

Skippering the Dons to European Cup Winners' Cup glory in Gothenburg naturally ranks as the highlight of his long and distinguished career; but on top of that, there is the European Super Cup, the full set of domestic trophies, numerous Dons appearance records and the winning of the Scottish Player of the Year award to be added, without even scratching the surface of Willie Miller's achievements.

In November 1989, tragedy struck, when, in a World Cup qualifier against Norway, Willie sustained a leg injury that was to effectively end his playing career. He did return to play a few games later that season and played his last game on 21st August 1990, a 2-1 Skol League Cup win at Queen's Park.

His playing days over, Willie remained at Pittodrie on the coaching staff, until a 1-0 defeat at home by Hibs on 8th February 1992 proved to be the straw that broke the camel's back as far as manager, Alex Smith, was concerned. He became the first Dons boss to be formally sacked by the club and into the breach stepped Willie.

Rangers were the bane of the Dons in Willie's first full season in charge, beating Aberdeen in both domestic cup finals and winning the league, with the Pittodrie side in the runners-up position.

A second place finish in the league the following season was followed by a disastrous run in 1994-95 and after a 3-1 reversal at Kilmarnock on 4th February, Willie became the second Dons boss to be formally sacked. He remains heavily involved in Scottish football through his work in the media.

JOHN McMASTER

riginally spotted as a winger playing for Port Glasgow Juniors, John was signed by Aberdeen in April 1972. He played for the top team for the first time on 24th August 1974, coming on as a substitute in the 3-0 win over Dunfermline Athletic.

It was not until the following season that John was given an extended run in the team and by this time he had been switched to a midfield berth, following some impressive performances in the reserves.

A classy player, with an uncanny ability to weight passes of any length, John also had a fierce shot and scored many a 'screamer' in his time.

John established himself as a first team regular in season 1977-78 and for the next three years he rarely missed a game, playing an important part in the title-winning campaign of 1979-80.

Sadly, John will remember the following season for all the wrong reasons. In a third round, first leg League Cup tie against Rangers at Ibrox on 3rd September 1980, he was injured in an ugly incident involving Willie Johnston, which could well have been a lot worse than it was.

Having recovered from that one, on 22nd October, in the European Cup second round, first leg Pittodrie clash with Liverpool, he was heavily downed by Ray Kennedy, sustaining a leg injury which would see him take no further part in that season's action.

Thankfully, John was able to recover in time for the next season and picked up a Scottish Cup winner's medal on 22nd May 1982, after the 4-1 extra time victory against Rangers.

For the European Cup Winners' Cup success season of 1982-83, John played for most of the time at left-back, a position to which he adapted effortlessly. That is where he starred for both the Gothenburg final and the Scottish Cup Final, a 1-0 success over Rangers.

After starting the next season at left-back, John lost his first team spot in October and for the next couple of seasons, his appearances at the top level were few and far between. However, a first team recall towards the end of the 1985-86 season saw John pick up an unexpected bonus in the twilight of his days as a Don - another Scottish Cup winner's medal in the 3-0 final win over Hearts on 10th May 1986.

John played only another twice for Aberdeen, his last match being the 5-0 league breeze against Clydebank at Pittodrie on 19th November 1986 and in February the following year, he was transferred to his home town team of Greenock Morton.

JIM LEIGHTON

Who could have predicted when twenty-year-old Jim made his first-team debut in a 4-1 Premier League win at Hearts on 12th August 1978, that he would still be involved at senior level into the next millennium?

Signed from junior club, Dalry Thistle the previous year, Jim played seventeen times during that season and two the following year, spending part of the time farmed out to Highland League club Deveronvale.

By the start of the 1980-81 campaign, Jim was the recognised first-team keeper at Pittodrie, missing only one league game that year, the 2-0 home win over Kilmarnock on 11th October 1980. His arrival, along with the likes of Willie Miller and Alex McLeish, coincided with the most successful period in the history of Aberdeen Football Club.

The Scottish Cup was lifted in season 1981-82 and retained for the next two seasons. The European Cup Winners' Cup was won in 1982-83, with the European Super Cup and the Scottish League Championship in 1983-84. The league was retained in 1984-85 and the Scottish Cup and Skol League Cup were lifted in 1985-86. All these honours were achieved with Jim between the sticks.

Although no further silverware was won in Jim's last couple of seasons in his first spell at Aberdeen, his form, particularly in season 1987-88, when he never missed a game, was superb and it was no real surprise when he followed his former boss, Alex Ferguson, to try his luck south of the border with Manchester United. By this time Jim had also established himself as the Scotland number one as well.

His career at Old Trafford was following a similar pattern to his Dons one, until he was very publicly dropped from the FA Cup Final replay in 1990 against Crystal Palace, after the 3-3 draw at Wembley.

There then followed the lowest spell of Jim's career with loan periods at Arsenal and Sheffield United, before an eventual transfer back to Scotland with Dundee, which proved to be disastrous.

Just when it looked as though Jim's career, would quietly disappear into the twilight, in stepped Hibs boss, Alex Miller, to take the keeper to Easter Road. It proved to be a masterstroke and with Jim's confidence completely restored, he was recalled by Scotland as well as performing miracles for the Hibees.

At the conclusion of the 1996-97 season, Jim was brought back to Aberdeen by boss, Roy Aitken, on a four-year deal. In his first year back, with his fortieth birthday approaching, he proved age was no barrier, with a string of consistently high-quality performances. That season ended with the emotion of the 1998 World Cup Finals in France.

The 1998-89 campaign was not such a happy one for Jim. In October 1998, he announced his retirement from the international scene and in February 1999, he lost his first-team spot.

However, with a year still remaining of his contract at time of writing, you can be sure you haven't heard the last of the Dons finest ever keeper!

ERIC BLACK

Eric arrived at Pittodrie straight from Alness Academy, Ross-shire, in 1980 and very quickly forged his way into the first team, becoming a first-team regular within a couple of years, whilst still a teenager.

The young striker made his debut in a 1-1 Pittodrie draw with 'New Firm' rivals, Dundee United, on 31st October 1981, taking a mere nine minutes to open the scoring, when he headed home a Gordon Strachan corner.

Renowned for his aerial ability, Eric was an extremely popular player with the fans and in that first season came on as a substitute in the 4-1 extra time Scottish Cup Final success against Rangers. He also made a scoring European debut, firing the opener in the 3-2 UEFA Cup third round, first leg win against SV Hamburg. The goal proved to be to no avail, however, with the Dons losing the return leg 3-1.

As was the case with so many of the squad of the time, it was the following season that was to turn out to be the high point of Eric's term with the Pittodrie club. On that wet evening of 11th May 1983, in Gothenburg, it was his shot that opened the scoring to send Aberdeen on the way to their most famous win ever, the 2-1 victory over Real Madrid in the European Cup Winners' Cup Final.

Ten days later, his immortality as a Don was complete, when he fired the only goal of the Scottish Cup Final at Hampden to leave Rangers in the runners-up spot for the second successive year.

A back injury with season 1983-84 just a few weeks old, turned out to be more serious than at first thought, although, happily, by the turn of the year, he was back and fit enough to play in most of the games during the second half of the season. His goals included, yet again, a Cup Final strike, this time in the 2-1 win over Celtic.

More success followed with the winning of the Scottish Premier League title in 1984-85 and a double in the Skol Cup Final of 1985-86, before boss, Alex Ferguson, dramatically omitted him from the Cup Final side to play Hearts in May 1986 because he had publicly stated he would be moving to Metz when his contract expired. The Dons lifted the Cup and Eric moved to France.

Eric enjoyed a successful spell with Metz, before injury forced him to retire when he should still have had many seasons left at the top. After a spell as an SFA Community Coach, he is currently on the coaching staff at Celtic.

THEO SNELDERS

**W**hen Theo joined the Dons from FC Twente in 1988, very few people in the Scottish game knew anything about him. Little did anyone realise the impact he would have at Aberdeen Football Club.

Jim Leighton had stunned everyone at Pittodrie when he joined Manchester United in the summer of 1988 and the new management team of Alex Smith and Jocky Scott had move quickly to secure a replacement with the £300,000 signing of the Dutch keeper.

Understandably, Theo had a lot to live up to, following in the footsteps of a man regarded as the finest goalkeeper ever to play at Pittodrie. Theo, however, had the Dons support questioning that fact in less than a season, with some incredible displays in goal. He capped a dream first season in Scotland by collecting the coveted Scottish Players' Player of the Year award.

The following season saw the big Dutchman go from strength to strength and also culminated in the Dons completing a cup double over the Old Firm. Having been defeated in the two previous League Cup Finals, the Dons headed into their third meeting with bitter rivals Rangers and it was a case of third time lucky, with Theo having a cracking game. He was again the hero in the Scottish Cup Final, where his tremendous penalty save from Anton Rogan helped the Dons secure the trophy over the other half of the Old Firm, Celtic.

Disaster struck the following year, when he was involved in a horrendous incident at rain-lashed Pittodrie against Rangers. Theo and Ally McCoist were racing for a 50-50 ball at the edge of the 18 yard box, when the Rangers striker slid in to challenge for the loose ball. The slippery conditions accelerated the slide and McCoist's boot caught Theo in the face. The diagnosis was a broken cheekbone and the keeper was sidelined for almost three months.

He returned to the starting line-up at the end of the year and played a huge part in the Dons' run at league leaders, Rangers. Again, though, disaster struck when a shoulder injury was sustained at Easter Road. He was to miss the remainder of the season and the infamous 'decider' at Ibrox.

Theo's Pittodrie career stalled from there and in 1995 the popular Dutchman left Pittodrie to join Rangers, where he featured in the first team sparingly. In the summer of 1999, he left Ibrox to return to his native Holland.

JOHN HEWITT

Forever remembered and quite rightly, too, for that goal in Gothenburg on 11th May 1983, Aberdeen born John contributed substantially more to the Dons than the most exhilarating moment in the club's history!

Signed from Middlefield Wasps in 1979, John was given an early first-team baptism, playing in the 2-0 league success against St Mirren on 15th December that same year.

In that inaugural season, he made five appearances, including three as a substitute and in the following year he turned out twenty-eight times, seventeen of which were from the bench.

Season 1981-82 witnessed the real arrival of John as a top-class forward and he played on forty-five occasions, only six of which were as a substitute. The Dons finished runners-up in the league that year and John bagged a memorable treble in the final game of the season, at home to Rangers on 15th May, a match that ended 4-0.

Seven days later he helped Aberdeen beat the same opponents at Hampden to lift the Scottish Cup with a 4-1 extra time victory.

The following season was, of course, the Cup Winners' Cup-winning one and John's influence throughout that campaign was very great. He scored two of the goals that saw off Sion of Switzerland in the 11-1 aggregate thumping, the only goal of the tie in the first round against the Albanians, Dinamo Tirana and then the remarkable winner against Bayern Munich in the quarter finals. All of that before coming off the bench on that wet night and heading the winner past Real Madrid keeper, Augustin, in the final.

A second Scottish Cup winner's medal followed on 21st May 1983, when he appeared as a sub as the Dons retained the trophy, again against Rangers.

Five days before Christmas that year, the European Super Cup was added, with victory over Hamburg, and later that season, a League winner's medal as the Dons completed the campaign with a Premier League record tally of fifty-seven points.

More success followed. The next season, John picked up a second League winner's medal, as Aberdeen retained the title with an even better points haul of fifty-nine and the following year, he was the Cup Final hero with a brace in the 3-0 victory against Hearts.

Although there were no trophies in 1986-87, John had the small consolation of finishing as joint top scorer, along with Billy Stark, with fourteen goals. John continued at Pittodrie until the summer of 1989, when he was transferred to rivals, Celtic, before moving to St Mirren via Highland League outfit Deveronvale.

EOIN JESS

Once on the books of Rangers as a schoolboy, Portsoy-born Eoin is the current darling of the Aberdeen support and (fingers crossed) he will end his playing days at Pittodrie.

His debut came on 6th May 1989 in a goalless home draw with Motherwell and less than six months later he was gracing Hampden, as Aberdeen lifted the Skol Cup after the 2-1 extra time success over Rangers. A month previously, Eoin had played in a European tie for the first time, in the 2-1 home UEFA Cup victory against Rapid Vienna, a tie which the Dons were to lose on the 'away' goals ruling.

One of the personal highlights for Eoin in season 1990-91 was the scoring of two hat-tricks. The first, on 24th November 1990, came at Tannadice and gave the visitors a 3-2 win over their 'New Firm' rivals. The second, at Dunfermline Athletic on 5th January 1991, was even more spectacular, with Eoin grabbing all four as the Pars were thumped 4-1 after taking an early lead.

Eoin ended that season as joint top scorer on fifteen with Dutchman, Hans Gillhaus and the following year he topped the scoring charts on his own, with twelve. Sadly, he was the only Don that particular year to reach double figures in what was a pretty wretched season.

The next year was very much a case of, 'so near and yet so far', with Rangers the thorn in the Dons' flesh at every turn. A 2-1 extra time defeat in the Skol Cup Final at Hampden on 25th October set the tone. The Dons finished runners-up to the Ibrox side in the League and lost to them at Parkhead on 29th May 1993 at the last stage of the Tennents Scottish Cup, in a game which saw Eoin come on as a substitute.

The most memorable aspects of the next two seasons was Aberdeen's bid to avoid relegation in 1994-95, a feat they eventually accomplished, only after being put through the agonies of a play-off against First Division Dunfermline.

On 26th November 1995 at Hampden, Eoin helped the Dons lift the, by then renamed, 'Coca-Cola Cup', with a 2-0 win over Dundee. It was not long after this that Eoin announced the intention of trying his luck in the Premiership and in February 1996 he was transferred to Coventry City for £1.7 million.

Sadly (although not for the Dons) his time in England was not a particularly happy one and in the summer of 1997, he returned to Pittodrie for around half the price he had been sold for. Following an indifferent start to his second spell as a Don, he at last began to display his exceptional talents on a consistent basis during 1998-89 to the extent that has now been recalled to the Scotland set-up.

DAVE ROBB

Born in 1947 in Broughty Ferry, Dave put pen to paper for the Dons in 1965, following a short spell down south with Chelsea. A player who could never be criticised for giving anything less than one hundred percent, Dave made his first Aberdeen appearance on 28th January 1967, in a 5-0 Scottish Cup first round success at Dundee.

By season 1968-69, Dave's was a regular name on the Dons team sheet and despite the occasional glaring miss in front of goal, was a great favourite with the fans because of his never-say-die attitude.

He played in all thirty-four league games the following season and in the Scottish Cup run, which culminated in the lifting of the trophy against Celtic on 11th April 1970, he scored three times, twice in the 4-0 first round win at home to Clyde and the decider in the 2-1 second round success against Clydebank at Pittodrie.

Dave's robust, not to mention pretty successful, approach brought him to the attention of the international selectors and in 1971 he earned five caps for Scotland.

In 1972 the bustling inside forward picked up a cartilage injury, which continued to cause problems for the remainder of his career. Being the type of player he was, however, he only did not play when absolutely forced and continued to notch up a creditable number of appearances, season after season.

One of his most memorable games for the Dons came in the League Cup Final meeting with Celtic on 6th November 1976, a game that started badly when the green and whites went ahead through an early Kenny Dalglish penalty. However, Drew Jarvie's leveller signalled extra time.

Dave was on the bench that day and had come on for goalscorer, Drew. Only three minutes of the additional period had elapsed when up he came to knock home what proved to be the winning goal, to give the Dons the trophy for the first time in twenty-one years.

In total, Dave played three hundred and forty-five times for the Dons, scoring ninety-eight goals in the process. His final outing was on 14th January 1978, when a 2-1 Pittodrie league win was recorded over Celtic. When he left Aberdeen, he spent a while involved in the United States soccer scene before signing for Norwich City.

DUNCAN SHEARER

Duncan Shearer's arrival at Pittodrie in the summer of 1992 signalled the birth of a new hero for the Red Army as, not since the days of Joe Harper, had the club seen such a prolific striker.

A native of Fort William, 'Dunc' joined the Dons from Blackburn Rovers, having made his name under Glenn Hoddle and Ossie Ardiles at Swindon. To say he had a good start to his Aberdeen career is putting it mildly.

A double on his debut announced his arrival and by the end of August, the flame-haired striker had scored eight goals. Come the end of that first season, he has added another twenty but unfortunately, the Dons had finished runners up to Rangers on all fronts.

The following season saw Aberdeen slip up in cup competitions and fall just short in the league yet again. This was made all the more frustrating by the fact that Rangers had suffered a topsyturvy season, yet the indifferent Dons had failed to capitalise. Again, Shearer had been a shining light, scoring 26 goals. However, the goalscoring prowess of the highlander had never been needed more.

Billy Dodds had arrived from St Johnstone and was seen as the perfect foil for Shearer. However, a dismal season saw the Dons slip to bottom of the table with three games remaining. In addition, Willie Miller had been fired and replaced by Roy Aitken.

Having led a resurrection of sorts, Aitken had steered his team back to within touching distance of Dundee United, who were due to visit Pittodrie. If the Dons had lost this game, they would have been relegated for the first time in the club's history. It was fitting, then, that Dodds had scored the opening goal and Shearer the second. Future Don, Robbie Winters, pulled one back just before full time but the home side held on. The atmosphere was electric and it's doubtful if the stadium will ever again see such dramatic scenes. The Dons won all their remaining games, including the two-leg play-off against Dunfermline Athletic, in which Shearer again played his part. Aberdeen were safe.

Having avoided relegation and now looking more like the Reds of old, Shearer received long overdue international recognition and scored in the Coca-Cola Cup Final to complete a remarkable turnaround in fortunes for all concerned with Aberdeen Football Club.

However, 'Old Father Time' was against Duncan and he soon became a bench player, making few appearances. In 1997, he joined Inverness Caledonian Thistle as a player with coaching duties and there, at time of writing, he remains.

BOBBY CLARK

ne of the first players signed under the 'Turnbull Revolution' of 1965, the popular goalkeeper was no stranger to Eddie Turnbull, the pair having worked together at Queen's Park.

Bobby took over from John 'Tubby' Ogston between the sticks, making his first appearance in a 2-0 League Cup win over Clyde on 28th August 1965 and very quickly established himself as a reliable, no-frills keeper, who instilled confidence in his defenders.

He also went on to be something of an institution at Pittodrie, notching up almost six hundred top-team appearances in a Dons career that lasted until the conclusion of the title winning 1979-80 season.

Within that fifteen-year span, there were plenty of highlights for Bobby to look back on with satisfaction, including the Scottish Cup success of 1969-70, the winning of the League Cup in 1976 and the lifting of the league just prior to his moving on.

There were also some less memorable times, particularly in seasons 1968-69 and 1969-70, when Bobby was vying for both the Dons and Scotland number one shirts with Ernie McGarr. Early on in the latter season, with McGarr between the sticks, Clark twice featured as an outfield player. He replaced Jim Forrest in a 2-0 defeat at Rangers and then played the whole match as the Dons went down 3-1 at St Johnstone.

Stoke City came very close to prizing Bobby away from Pittodrie in 1972 after the keeper, disillusioned as the Dons were going through a poor patch, put in a transfer request. For their part, City were seeking a replacement for Gordon Banks, who had suffered terrible injuries in that infamous car crash and a move seemed certain.

However, at the last minute, Stoke reduced their offer for Bobby from the anticipated £100,000 to just £60,000 and the deal fell through. Stoke's loss was Aberdeen's gain and Bobby went on to give many more seasons of sterling service.

On leaving Pittodrie, Bobby moved to Clyde for a short spell before moving into coaching, initially in Africa and then at Dartmouth College in the United States. From there, Bobby enjoyed a spell as the New Zealand national coach before returning to America with Stanford University, where he remains at present, as one of the most respected figures in the game in his adopted country.

DEAN WINDASS

One of the more colourful characters to grace Pittodrie in recent times, many fans would include 'Deano' in their list of legends. His Dons exit was not the most glorious, however, and he was allowed to go to Oxford by then boss Alex Miller. The Englishman is currently back down south with Bradford in the Premiership.

WILLIE COOPER

Signed from local junior side, Mugiemoss, in June 1927, full back Willie made his Dons debut in a 3-0 home win over Cowdenbeath on 14th April 1928, although it wasn't until the 1930-31 season that he made the right back position his own.

Willie was one of those players who always seemed to manage to steer clear of injury and between September 1932 and October 1936, he set a new club record for consecutive league matches, notching up an unbroken run of a hundred and thirty-two games.

Not a player who liked to venture overly far up the field, preferring to stick to his main task of preventing the opposition from scoring, he managed just three goals in his three hundred and seventy-three appearances for the Pittodrie club. Two of those came within a few weeks of one another, in league matches against Cowdenbeath and Clyde, in early 1933.

The third came after a gap of fourteen years, in the Scottish Cup first round match against Partick Thistle, a game won 2-1 by the Dons. That victory was the start on the road to Hampden that season, although, cruelly for someone who kept himself so clear of problems, a muscle strain prevented him from playing in the final and being a member of the first Aberdeen side to lift the Scottish Cup.

There was a small consolation for Willie. In the light of his contribution to Aberdeen's run to the final and indeed, to the club itself, the SFA sanctioned the striking of a special medal for him, a rare concession in those days.

Willie continued to play the following season, with his final match for Aberdeen being on 31st January 1948, three months short of twenty years since he had made his debut. It was, sadly, not to be a winning sign off and an Archie Kelly goal was not sufficient to prevent Falkirk recording a 3-1 win at Brockville.

At the conclusion of that season, one of the most loyal servants ever to have played for Aberdeen finally left Pittodrie to move to pastures new, taking up the position of player-manager with Huntly in the Highland League, where he went on to star for several years before at last hanging up his boots.

JACK ALLISTER

Instantly remembered by more mature Dons supporters as the right half who formed part of the legendary 1954-55 title-winning half-back line of Allister, Young and Glen, ex-paratrooper Jack was originally an inside forward when he was signed from Chelsea by manager, Dave Halliday, in the autumn of 1952.

In his six seasons at Pittodrie, Jack made 163 appearances for Aberdeen, finding the net on twenty-four occasions, sixteen of which were from the penalty spot. The Edinburgh-born player, who had started his football career with Tranent Juniors before moving south in 1949, was an extremely dependable player and good in the tackle. He would have played more times for the Pittodrie side had a couple of injuries not kept him out of action for lengthy spells.

Jack played his final game for Aberdeen on the 18th January 1958, an uneventful 1-1 draw with Celtic on a snowbound Parkhead, in which Dickie Ewen was on target for the visitors.

Off the field, Jack was generally regarded as one of the quiet men of Pittodrie, although the perception belied the reality, as he was very much the life and soul of the party at any social occasion.

After leaving the Dons, Jack enjoyed a spell in the Highland League with Deveronvale and down south with Chesterfield, where he became a good friend of former England keeper, Gordon Banks. After hanging up his boots, Jack spent a number of years in Australia before returning to his native Edinburgh, where he reluctantly again took up his original trade as a plumber.

Jack was forced to give up plumbing after suffering a severe heart attack and for eight years worked at the Lord Roberts Workshop for the Disabled, along with other former servicemen.

Sadly, Jack's health was never fully restored and after a long illness, in the early part of 1999, he died in his home city. With his passing, another link with that great Championship winning side of 1955 was lost.

CHRIS ANDERSON

lthough his most significant contribution to the club he grew up, quite literally in the shadows of, came after he joined the Board in the 1960s, Chris Anderson was an accomplished half back who spent five seasons as a first-team player at Pittodrie between 1948-49 and 1952-53.

The Scottish schoolboy internationalist was snapped up from local side, Mugiemoss, during the Second World War and made his debut on New Year's Day 1949, co-incidentally in the same game as Jackie Hather made his first top-team appearance. Sadly, his opening game was not a happy one, with the Dons going down 3-1 at home to high-flying Dundee.

By the following season, Chris was well established at Pittodrie and in a memorable Scottish Cup third round tie in Glasgow on 25th February 1950, he scored the only goal of the game to give the Dons their first ever victory at Parkhead in the national competition.

Early the following year, Chris' performances had come to the attention of the national selectors and he was chosen in the squad for a Scottish League match. Unfortunately, fate took a hand and he was forced to withdraw from the pool when he picked up a knee injury in a 4-3 win at Celtic on 13th January 1951. To complete what turned out to be a miserable afternoon, Chris managed to put through his own net prior to sustaining the knock.

At the conclusion of the 1952-53 season, Chris was transferred to Arbroath, having found his first-team chances limited by the form of Tony Harris in the right half position.

During season 1956-57, he hung up his boots to concentrate on his business interests, his last appearance for the Red Lichties being a Scottish Cup tie against Rothes. Ten years later, he was back at Pittodrie, this time as a director, where his vision and business acumen paved the way forward, not just for Aberdeen but also for the game in Scotland as a whole.

Chris Anderson was one of the leading lights behind the formation of the Scottish Premier League and a man who, along with then Chairman, Dick Donald, was responsible for putting the infrastructure into place to enable the Dons to become such a force in Europe in the eighties.

His untimely death in 1986 resulted in Scottish football losing one of its most respected figures and in the case of Aberdeen, a man who, quite literally, would be impossible to replace.

MIXU PAATELAINEN

Another player who had a loyal band of followers during his time with Aberdeen, the Finnish international came to Pittodrie from neighbours Dundee United. Following a spell in England, Mixu is back in the top flight in Scotland with Hibs.

ALLY SHEWAN

Ally joined Aberdeen from Formartine United in 1960 and played reserve team football until he made the breakthrough to the first team in 1963. Once there, he passed Willie Cooper's pre-war record of 162 consecutive first-team appearances! Playing in what was a disappointing era for the Pittodrie club, Ally stood out and his displays at the heart of the Dons defence are still remembered today.

A big strapping defender, he made his debut for the Pittodrie club against Motherwell on 23rd March 1963. Ally was very much the 'enforcer' of the Dons back line and always took the simple option. His never-say-die attitude served him well, with many a timely interception saving the day for the Dons and not surprisingly, he became a big favourite with the Pittodrie faithful.

Arguably, the 1967 season was Ally's finest in the red of Aberdeen and is one on which many older Dons fans look back with great affection, despite the season ending on a barren note.

Eddie Turnbull had taken over the managerial position at Pittodrie in 1965 and made the headlines by transfer-listing seventeen members of the playing staff.

He set about building a new side, of which Ally was an integral component. The Pittodrie supporters were desperate for some success following the disappointing seasons they had endured, with the Dons failing to finish in the top five for the best part of a decade.

A semi-final replay defeat at the hands of Rangers in the League Cup suggested the Dons were improving and come Christmas, Turnbull's Dons were occupying second place in the league – with Ally playing a big part.

The second half of the season saw the Dons' league challenge falter but a storming Scottish Cup run brought them to their first final in eight years and it was twenty years since they had last won it.

Turnbull took ill on the eve of the final and his players were forced to battle on by themselves. As brave as Ally and his team-mates were, they couldn't overcome the soon to be European Champions and Celtic ran out two-goal winners.

Celtic, however, had won the League Championship, which meant they had to vacate their Cup Winner's Cup place. This meant Ally and his team-mates were set for the first ever European match.

The Dons continued to struggle and in 1969 Ally left Pittodrie for St George's Budapest in Sydney. He lasted a week before returning to Scotland with Elgin City, where he played for many years.

MATT ARMSTRONG

C entre forward, Matt Armstrong, arrived at Pittodrie just before the start of season 1931-32, after being released by Celtic but although he made the occasional appearance in the first team during his first three years with the Dons, it was 1934-35 before he established himself as a regular, forming a superb understanding with Willie Mills.

Port Glasgow-born Matt finished as Pittodrie's top scorer in each of the next four seasons and his form not surprisingly earned him a Scotland call-up. The Scottish Cup campaign of season 1936-37 was to prove to be a watershed, as Aberdeen at last made it through to a Hampden final, thanks in no small measure to the goals of Matt.

A treble in the first round thumping of Inverness Thistle was followed by strikes in both the quarter and semi finals against Hamilton Accies and Morton respectively.

The Dons had reached Hampden for the first time, after six failures at the semi final stage and on 24th April 1937, a crowd of more than a hundred and forty-six thousand packed into the national stadium to watch the game against Celtic.

After Celtic had taken the early lead, it was Matt who led the immediate response by firing home the equaliser. Unfortunately, however, their first major final was not to be the 'Black and Golds' day and in the second half, Celtic scored what proved to be the winner.

The outbreak of World War II ensured the Cup Final outing was to be the highlight of Matt's time with Aberdeen. Although he did turn out for the Dons during the hostilities, he spent a short while with Queen of the South before returning to the north as player-coach with Elgin City.

When he hung up his boots, Matt worked as a car salesman before retiring to live in Cults. In his later years he remained a keen follower of the Dons and was a regular visitor at Pittodrie, still recognised by the more mature fraternity within the Red Army.

ARCHIE BAIRD

lthough inside-forward, Archie Baird, was signed by Aberdeen in 1938, the intervention of World War II meant that it was season 1946-47 before he received his first taste of 'proper' top team action, that coming after spending a slice of the hostilities as a P.O.W. in Italy.

Although 'official' matches did not restart until that 1946-47 season, it is also worth noting that no less than 135,000 fans packed into Hampden in May 1946 for the final of the Southern League Cup between the Dons and Rangers, a game in which Archie opened the scoring to set up a 3-2 Aberdeen victory.

His first 'official' game was in a 3-0 win away to now defunct Third Lanark, a game notable on a couple of counts. Firstly, it was played at Hampden Park due to the fact that Cathkin Park was unplayable and secondly, the Dons wore their then change colours of blue (that would never be acceptable these days!).

In his second outing for Aberdeen, Archie fired the goal of the game to defeat Kilmarnock at Pittodrie, before going on to find the net seven times in nineteen games during his inaugural season with the Dons.

The highlight of that first season was, of course, the lifting of the Scottish Cup for the first time ever, with a, 2-1 Hampden success over Hibs, in which Archie certainly played his part as the team from the Granite City captured the much sought-after silverware.

Undoubtedly, Archie would have notched up far more than the thirty-seven goals he did manage in a hundred and forty-four games, had it not been for a string of injury worries, most notably cartilage problems.

Archie was transferred to St Johnstone at the conclusion of the 1952-53 season, ending an association with the Dons which had stretched back fifteen years. A change of position to wing-half with the Perth club saw Archie enjoy a real Indian summer before hanging up his boots for good.

Away from football, Archie's other claim to fame was that he was the brother-in-law of Mastermind presenter, Magnus Magnusson, whilst, in his fifties, he was awarded an honours degree in Italian, a language that had continued to fascinate him since his wartime experiences and which he had always promised himself he would learn to speak fluently.

HENNING BOEL

This talented Danish international defender joined Aberdeen in November 1968 from the club whose name the Dons had temporarily borrowed on the American tour the previous year, the Washington Whips.

Henning made his Dons debut on 4th January 1968 in a 4-1 league win at Tannadice and played in all of the Dons' remaining games that season. A classy player who combined tremendous tackling ability with a great turn of speed, Henning would press forward at every available opportunity, though he only found the net four times during his Aberdeen career.

An outstanding performance in the Scottish Cup Final win over Celtic in season 1969-70 was, not surprisingly, overshadowed somewhat by the scoring exploits of one Derek 'cup-tie' McKay. His double in the match was the stuff of dreams but it's fair to say that Henning and his defensive colleagues more than played their role in ensuring the return of silverware to the 'Granite City'.

The following season saw Henning in and out of the first team before beginning 1972-73 in fine fashion. The Dane had missed only a couple of League Cup ties when the Dons travelled to Germany to face Borussia Moenchen-Gladbach in the second leg of their opening round UEFA Cup tie, having lost out 3-2 at Pittodrie.

Early in the match, Henning was stretchered off the park, having sustained the bad knee injury that would effectively end his career as a Don. As for the game itself, a tremendous performance saw Aberdeen 3-2 up at the interval, 5-5 the aggregate score, before the Germans rallied to find the net four times after the break.

Henning recovered sufficiently to play the last few games that season and then a handful of games in the 1973-74 campaign, his final outing as Don coming in a rather insipid 1-1 Pittodrie draw against Clyde, in which Drew Jarvie's opener was cancelled out in injury time by Willie McVie.

On leaving Aberdeen in 1974, Henning, who was married to an American girl, lived in the States for a while. At time of writing, he is back in his native Denmark, where he is working for a company that manufactures training footballs.

MARTIN BUCHAN

Called up by Eddie Turnbull from Banks O'Dee 'A', where he had been farmed out, in time for the start of the 1966-67 season, the local youngster, whose father had also played for Aberdeen, made his debut in October 1966 at the tender age of seventeen.

The game, a 1-1 draw at Dunfermline, in which Ally Shewan grabbed a last-minute leveller, was notable not just for the fact Martin made his debu, but also because skipper, Harry Melrose, was red-carded. The teenager was used sparingly in that first season, playing on just four occasions, although he was included in the squad for the Scottish Cup Final, a game won 2-0 by Celtic.

By the start of the next season, Martin was an automatic first choice for the Dons and he played thirty-four times. For 1968-69, his appearances increased to more than forty and it was during the following season, in February 1970 and not yet twenty-one, that Martin received the honour of being made team captain.

Within two months of his elevation, Martin was celebrating being the youngest ever captain of a Scottish Cup-winning side, as the Dons swept aside odds-on favourite, Celtic, 3-1 at Hampden. More than fifty thousand lined the streets of Aberdeen on the team's return.

By now, Martin, one of the country's classiest young defenders, was a firm favourite with the Red Army, whilst his progress was being monitored enviously by a host of top clubs.

Nineteen seventy-one saw the Dons' skipper pick up the accolade of Scottish Player of the Year and win the first of his thirty-four international caps. Having been at the top in Scotland, Martin now fancied trying his luck south of the border and in February 1972, much to the dismay of the Aberdeen fans, he was transferred to Manchester United for a fee of £125,000.

Martin spent eleven seasons at Old Trafford, winning the FA Cup in 1977, before moving on to Oldham. A brief and none-too-successful foray into the world of management followed at Burnley, before Martin decided that his future lay away from football.

Not that he remained that far removed from the game, spending a considerable time working for the current manufacturers of the Aberdeen kit before leaving the company in 1999. The family name, of course, lives on at Pittodrie, with Martin's son, Scottish under-21 international, Jamie, very much part of the first-team squad.

PADDY BUCKLEY

Signed at the conclusion of the 1951-52 season for a fee of £7,500 from St. Johnstone, one of the fastest players in the country in his time made his debut on 9th August 1952 in a League Cup tie at Motherwell.

Although he took just eighteen minutes to open his account with the Dons, it proved not to be a happy first match, with the Fir Park side running out easy 5-2 victors. Incidentally, another player to make his first appearance that day was former Morton full back, Jimmy Mitchell.

A height of only 5' 6" belied an ability to leap like the proverbial salmon, as many a defender found to his cost and in his five seasons at Pittodrie, he amassed a very creditable total of ninety-two goals in a hundred and fifty-two games.

One match in particular ensured Paddy's immortality in the eyes of the Aberdeen support of the fifties and that was on 10th April 1954, when the Dons faced favourites, Rangers, in the semi-final of the Scottish Cup.

True, the Ibrox side were in the middle of a crisis of confidence. But the 'Gers were the holders of the trophy and certainly, not even the most ardent Dons fan could have expected that the Glasgow side were about to be given their biggest ever defeat in the competition.

Joe O'Neil led the assault with a treble, whilst Graham Leggat, a Jack Allister penalty and finally, a header from Paddy, brought about an incredible final score of 6-0 in front of a mainly shell-shocked crowd of 111,000 at Hampden Park.

Sadly, as most readers will be aware, Aberdeen could not repeat the performance in the final against the other half of the 'Old Firm' as, despite Paddy's well-taken goal in the 51st minute, the Dons lost the game 2-1.

Paddy was the Dons' top scorer, with twenty-eight goals, the following season, when, of course, the League Championship was lifted for the first time ever. The only disappointment for Paddy was that injury forced him to sit out the 1-0 win at Clyde that clinched the title. That was particularly hard on him, as he had fired a memorable treble the previous week in a 4-0 win over Rangers.

The Leith-born forward continued with Aberdeen for another couple of seasons before a bad knee injury forced him to quit, his final game being the 4-0 home win over St Mirren on 5th January 1957.

DONALD COLMAN

O n the face of it, the signing of Donald Colman by manager, Jimmy Philip, in 1907 seemed a strange one. At twenty-nine, he was not exactly in the first flush of youth, whilst his senior career, two inauspicious seasons at Motherwell before being freed, was hardly inspiring.

However, the capture of the Renton-born defender turned out to be a masterstroke of the highest order and Donald went on to become captain of the club and at the age of thirty-three, the oldest Aberdeen player to receive a national call-up.

Strangely, Colman was not Donald's real surname. He was born Donald Cunningham but used the alias to prevent his father from discovering he was playing the sport he had been forbidden from taking up.

When the First World War intervened in 1914, most people, understandably, thought that would be the last Aberdeen Football Club would see of Donald as a player. Not so! Following the cessation of hostilities, he was back at Pittodrie and still playing first-team football in 1920, at the age of forty-two.

On leaving Aberdeen at the end of the 1919-20 season, he became player-manager at Dumbarton and was still turning out for the Boghead side five years later.

However, that was by no means the end of Donald's involvement with Aberdeen Football Club and in 1931 manager, Paddy Travers, brought him back as trainer to succeed the late Billy Russell.

It is Donald, believe it or not, who is credited with inventing the soon-to-be ubiquitous trainer's dugout, with Pittodrie boasting what was very probably the first one in the world. In the thirties, when Everton played a friendly in Aberdeen, they immediately copied the idea and thus Goodison became the first English ground to boast such a facility.

Improving the game became almost an obsession with Donald and in the wake of the death of Celtic keeper, John Thomson, following the accidental collision with Rangers forward, Sam English, he came up with the idea of protective headgear for goalkeepers. In the event, this proved impractical, due to the weight of the contraption.

Donald remained at Pittodrie until the outbreak of the Second World War and this time, sadly, there was to be no going back. In 1942, at the age of sixty-four, Donald Colman, a man whose career began late and then became the stuff of dreams, died of tuberculosis.

MIKE NEWELL

The likable England 'B' international, who won a Premiership Winner's medal with Blackburn Rovers, was in the twilight of his career when he came to Aberdeen and played his part for a couple of seasons before being released towards the end of 1998-99. Now player-coach with non-league Doncaster.

CHARLIE COOKE

**F**ife-born Charlie was one of the many gems originally unearthed by that legend of the scouting world, Bobby Calder, who spotted the winger turning defences inside out playing for Renfrew Juniors.

Signed in October 1959, he was one of three teenagers to make his debut in a 4-3 League Cup success at home to Ayr United on August 13th 1960, the others being Des Herron and Doug Coutts.

A Scottish winger in the traditional mould, with the ability to beat defences on his own, Charlie was with Aberdeen until December 1964, scoring thirty times in a hundred and sixty-five appearances. His final goal came in his last game, a 6-3 thumping by league leaders, Hearts, on 12th December. After the match, Charlie was sold to Dundee for £40,000, a then record fee between two Scottish clubs.

The fact that Charlie had been such a star playing in an Aberdeen team which, to be honest, was struggling, to say the least, says much for his abilities. Just how successful he might have gone on to be, had he been part of an Aberdeen line-up from a different time, we will, of course, never know. However, the fact that, on signing him, Bobby Calder telephoned Pittodrie to say, "I've signed the greatest ball player you have ever seen", gives a fair indication of what the answer might be.

Within a couple of weeks, Charlie was back at Pittodrie, playing his part in a 1-1 draw between the Dons and Dundee. He did not have a particularly fruitful time of it that day but the following season saw Charlie scoring against his former team mates.

Although Charlie had won under-23 caps when with Aberdeen, it was during his spell on Tayside that he picked up full international honours. Within a couple of years, Dundee almost doubled their money when they transferred Charlie to Chelsea for £72,000.

Charlie went on to become a huge hit at Stamford Bridge, before moving across London to Crystal Palace in the autumn of 1972. Two years later, he returned to Chelsea, before moving across the pond to end his playing career in the United States.

Charlie's international haul of sixteen Scottish caps was significantly less than his abundant talents deserved. A real artist with a football, many Aberdeen supporters felt it was criminal to sell their prime asset to a rival club, particularly when, in this case, they very quickly made a huge profit on him.

JOE HARPER

hilst all Dons fans would have their own ideas as to who should feature in an all-time top fifty players who have graced Pittodrie, the Greenock-born 'King' would surely be one of the first inclusions in each and every list.

Arriving at Pittodrie from Morton in October 1969, Joe made his first appearance on the 4th of that month in a 2-1 victory at Ayr United. At Pittodrie seven days later, he scored the first of his hundred and ninety-one goals for Aberdeen, his penalty proving to be decisive in the 2-1 success over Partick Thistle.

Another penalty in the 1970 Scottish Cup Final, assured his place in the hearts of Dons fans for all time and over the next two seasons, he ended both campaigns as Aberdeen's top scorer, including an incredible forty-two goals in forty-seven outings in 1971-72, a feat which earned him the European 'Bronze Boot' for that particular season.

In December 1972, Joey was sold to Everton for a fee of £180,000, having already notched twenty-seven goals that season. It was a move which did not go down at all well with the fans, who were quick to voice their displeasure.

The move south did not work out as planned, although the Merseysiders' insistence on playing the burly hitman out of position did not help matters, and after little more than a year, he returned to Scotland with Hibs.

His time at Easter Road was not a particularly happy one and at the conclusion of season 1975-76, one which saw the Dons escape relegation by a whisker, the Red Army received the news it had longed for - 'King Joey' was coming home!

Unlike many other examples of players who have returned to former clubs and it hasn't worked out, Joe's second spell at Aberdeen was an unqualified success and he was top scorer for the next three seasons, with tallies of twenty-eight, twenty-seven and thirty-two!

An injury in a League Cup tie at Parkhead on 24th November 1979 all but ended Joe's playing career. The Dons were to go and win the league title that season and manager, Alex Ferguson, questioned whether they would have done so, had Joe been fit. 'Joey' made his final appearance for Aberdeen on the last day of the 1980-81 season in a 2-0 home defeat by already relegated Kilmarnock, to bringing the curtain down on a truly remarkable career.

Surprisingly, Joe was only capped four times for Scotland. On leaving the Dons, he was involved in the Highland League for some time. He is currently back at Morton, his first senior club, in the capacity of Commercial Manager.

FRED MARTIN

hilst many outfield players have been forced into making a temporary transition to goalkeeper, usually because of an injury, the story of Fred Martin is a remarkable one.

Signed as an inside-forward from Carnoustie Panmure in October 1946, it was during his National Service that Fred realised he had a natural talent for operating between the sticks. Consequently, the Dons lost a forward and two years later, gained a goalkeeper.

Fred made his debut on 14th April 1950, in a 3-1 defeat at East Fife, in which he spoiled a promising debut by dropping the ball into his own net in the last minute for a bizarre own goal.

From the beginning of season 1950-1 onwards, Fred was the undisputed number one at Pittodrie. And although the early fifties was not exactly the most successful of times at Aberdeen Football Club, his consistently good performances caught the eye.

He was chosen to play for the Scottish League in 1952 and two years later became a full international, earning a total of six caps and participating in the World Cup Finals of 1954.

His first real opportunity of picking up honours at club level came when the Dons reached the Scottish Cup Final in season 1952-53. Unfortunately, it was not to be and after a 1-1 draw in the first match, the plucky Dons were defeated by a single goal in the replay on 29th April 1953.

Twelve months later, Fred and the Dons were back at Hampden but once again had to settle for the runners-up spot, as this time Celtic lifted the trophy.

However, patience is a great virtue and at the conclusion of season 1954-55, Fred was the proud owner of a league winner's medal, having played in all but three of the matches that season, missing one through flu and two because of international duty.

From season 1956-57 onwards, Fred's career was beset by injury, with Reggie Morrison his normal deputy. In the three years commencing 1957-58, Fred managed less than forty starts, although by the time he announced his retirement in 1960, the big keeper had amassed two hundred and ninety one games for the Reds.

Fred's last game was on 16th January 1960, when he looked somewhat rusty in the early stages of the Pittodrie clash with Airdrie, gifting the Diamonds a couple of goals in the opening twenty-five minutes. Aberdeen fought back, though, with strikes from Jack Hather and Jim Clunie salvaging a valuable share of the spoils.

DON EMERY

One of the most powerful strikers of a dead ball ever seen at Pittodrie, Don came to Aberdeen from Swindon Town during the summer of 1948, in a deal which saw Andy Cowie moving in the opposite direction. Don's willingness to move to the 'Granite City' was down to the fact that his Aberdonian wife, Maude, was homesick and tired of living so far away from her family and friends.

The former Welsh schoolboy international made his debut on 14th August 1948 in a disappointing single goal defeat at the hands of Third Lanark and in his first season, was utilised both as a full back and a centre forward. In fact, it was Don's inclusion as a forward, due in part to injuries to George Hamilton and Archie Kelly, which was partially responsible for the mini revival that helped Aberdeen beat the drop that season.

In his ten league games at number nine, the diminutive Welshman averaged a goal every other game and in those matches, the Dons lost only twice.

The next season saw Don back in a more familiar role, as far as Aberdeen fans were concerned, at the back and he played forty games that season, ending up as the Pittodrie side's third-top-scorer, with nine. That haul included a smattering of spot kicks (all of them hit with a force resembling a cannonball!), as well as a cracker of a free kick in a 1-1 Pittodrie draw with Rangers in September 1949.

Don played thirty-seven times during the next season, all at full-back, and then thirty during 1951-52. Sadly, these were not the greatest of times for Aberdeen and the closest Don came to collecting any kind of honour was in 1950, when the Dons were beaten by Hibs in the quarter final of the League Cup, after extra time in a replay.

At the conclusion of season 1951-52, Don was allowed to move to East Fife, becoming part of the victorious team that lifted the League Cup in season 1953-54. At Methil, he became a team-mate of future Pittodrie boss, Jimmy Bonthrone, and was still destined to bag one more goal on his former stamping ground, converting a penalty for East Fife in a 5-1 League Cup defeat on 4th September 1954.

JIM FORREST

Glasgow born Jim joined Rangers straight from school in 1960 and did not take long to establish himself as a clinical finisher who could score with either foot. His goal scoring form soon attracted the attention of the national selectors and in 1965 he won what was to be the first of five caps.

However, Jim was one of several players at Ibrox who was to pay a heavy price for the ignominy of the Scottish Cup defeat at the hands of Berwick Rangers and was soon offloaded to Preston North End. His stay at Deepdale was a short one and the following year he signed for the Dons for £20,000.

His first outing in a red shirt came on 24th August 1968 and was not an inspiring one with Aberdeen losing 4-1 at Clyde in a League Cup sectional tie. In his second match he fired the only goal of the game in a win against Dunfermline Athletic. That first season was a poor one for Aberdeen although one game did give the former Ger personal satisfaction.

That came in the opening round of the Scottish Cup on 25th January 1969 when a brace from Jim helped the Dons to a 3-0 stroll against none other than….. Berwick Rangers.

His second season with the Dons was, of course, far more memorable with the lifting of the Scottish Cup the major highlight. Jim played in all of the games in that famous run, finding the net in the 2-1 victory over Clydebank in the second round.

At the start of the following campaign, Jim was moved wide right to allow Joe Harper to play through the middle. It was a move which was to pay dividends with a recall to the national side in 1971 after several seasons absence.

Jim continued as a regular in the Aberdeen line up until 1972-73 when he flitted in and out of the team. His final appearance was in a 1-1 draw at Arbroath on the 14th April 1973 when he was substituted by Bertie Miller. Unfortunately the occasion will be remembered not so much for the fact that it was Jim's farewell, but more because Bertie had forgotten to put his shorts on when he trotted on to Gayfield.

After his spell with Aberdeen, Jim moved to the Far East where he became one of a number of Scottish players to try their luck over there, in Jim's case with Hong Kong Rangers.

ARCHIE GLEN

In 1947, at the age of eighteen, a young inside forward was spotted playing for Ayrshire junior outfit, Annbank United. The youngster went on to become a lynchpin for Aberdeen Football Club during the fifties, whilst the man who 'discovered' him, George Hamilton, was destined to become one of his team-mates.

Archie Glen made his debut on 19th February 1949 in a 2-1 success at Falkirk but because of National Service, his appearances in the first team during his first few seasons at Pittodrie were limited, and it was not until 1953-54 that he really established himself.

And establish himself he certainly did, forming a third of the classic half back line of Allister, Young and Glen, reckoned by many to be the Dons' best ever.

Archie was an ever-present throughout the Dons' league title-winning campaign of 1954-55 and it was wholly appropriate that his spot kick, in the 13th minute of the game at Clyde on the 9th April 1955, finally secured the inaugural title for the Dons.

Appointed club captain the next year, Archie was an inspirational figure as the Dons went through a difficult period in the second half of the nineteen-fifties. In 1956 he was selected to play for Scotland twice, picking up caps for games against England and Northern Ireland. In addition, he was chosen to play for the Scottish League on six occasions.

A superstitious player, who always liked to be last out of the dressing room, Archie played his last game for Aberdeen on 23rd April 1960, in a 3-1 win at Arbroath on the penultimate Saturday of the season. It was an important victory, as well, as the result ensured the Dons' safety in the top flight following another poor campaign. Indeed, the Dons had four wins out of four in their final quartet of matches to thank for their survival.

Having been thirteen years with the Dons and now into his early thirties, Archie decided to bow out at the top and in the close season announced his retirement. If you asked any Aberdeen supporter who watched his heroes throughout the fifties, which player is most representative of that particular era, you can be sure the name of Archie Glen will be right up there among the top answers.

ARTHUR GRAHAM

Yet another great player the Dons have the late Bobby Calder to thank for finding, Arthur was brought up in the giant Castlemilk housing scheme in Glasgow and was discovered playing for Cambuslang Rangers.

Within a few months of arriving in the North East, the seventeen- year old found himself thrown in at the deep end by boss Eddie Turnbull, coming on as a substitute for Derek McKay in a 2-0 win over Dunfermline on 21st March 1970.

Three weeks later the fairytale was complete, when 'Bumper' was handed the number eleven shirt for the Scottish Cup Final meeting with Celtic. The youngster was by no means overawed by the enormity of the occasion and played his part in the 3-1 win.

For the next seven seasons, Arthur was almost an ever-present on the left wing for Aberdeen, making over three hundred appearances, in which he scored forty-six times. He picked up a League Cup winner's medal in 1976 when the Dons defeated Celtic 2-1 in the final, that coming after the famous 5-1 semi-final victory over the other half of the 'Old Firm'.

Among Arthur's goals, two worthy of special note were the couple he notched in Europe. On 16th September 1970, he fired the opener in the 3-1 Pittodrie win over Honved of Hungary in the first round of the Cup Winners' Cup. Unfortunately, it was exactly the reverse scoreline in the second leg and Aberdeen had to endure the agony of being dismissed on penalty kicks.

His other European strike came three years later, almost to the day, in the 4-1 UEFA Cup first round, first leg win over Irish outfit Finn Harps, a tie that saw the Dons progress 7-2 on aggregate, only to be eliminated by Tottenham Hotspur in the next round.

Recognised at Under-23 and Scottish League levels during his time at Pittodrie, Arthur was transferred south to Leeds United for a fee of £125,000 in the summer of 1977, his last game for the Dons being the 2-1 win over Rangers on 30th April that year.

Arthur spent six seasons at Elland Road and whilst there, picked up ten full international caps, the first coming in 1978. He then moved to Manchester United in 1983, spending a couple of years at Old Trafford, before joining Bradford City.

GEORGE HAMILTON

**O**ne of the many stars through the years to have cut his teeth in the world of junior football in Ayrshire, George was born in Irvine, making his name with local side, Meadow.

He moved to Queen of the South in the summer of 1937, spending a year with the Doonhamers, before being sold to the Dons for what was then a club record fee of £3,000. He made his debut on 13th August 1938 and in his first season, George proved that paying so much for his services was hardly a gamble, topping the scoring charts with eighteen goals in forty-two appearances.

His career, like so many of his generation, was then interrupted by the outbreak of hostilities. He returned to Aberdeen on the resumption of peace, playing in the 'unofficial' 3-2 League Cup Final win over Rangers in May 1946.

The following April saw George back at Hampden again, this time firing Aberdeen's equaliser in the 2-1 success over Hibs that gave the Dons the Scottish Cup for the first time in their history. The fact that George also saw a second-half spot kick saved by Hibs keeper, Kerr, fortunately did not matter in the end and the Dons held out for a well deserved win.

December 1947 saw George transferred to Hearts, as part of the deal that took Archie Kelly to Aberdeen but within six months he was back in the North East, where he was to spend a further seven seasons.

In his career, George played five times for his country, the last being in 1954, at the age of thirty-six. Ironically, by the time the League Championship-winning season of 1954-55 came around, he had become a 'squad' player although he did play four league matches that season, scoring twice.

Fittingly, his final game for the Dons came in the one that clinched the title, on 9th April 1955 at Shawfield, when that clinically struck penalty from Archie Glen secured the first ever title. That appearance earned George the distinction of being the only player to be present when Aberdeen celebrated both major domestic 'firsts', namely the League and the Scottish Cup.

In the summer of 1955, George moved to Hamilton Accies, where he spent just six months before finally hanging up his boots.

JACK HATHER

Englishman, Jack Hather, first wore an Aberdeen shirt on New Year's Day 1949, having signed a month earlier, on the same day Chris Anderson celebrated his debut. Not that a 3-1 home defeat by Dundee was much to celebrate!

During his first few seasons at Pittodrie, most of his time was spent in the reserves as understudy to future manager, Tommy Pearson. Having said that, by the time he became the first-choice left winger at the start of the 1952-53 season, he had already amassed sixty-three first team appearances.

For the remainder of the fifties, Jack was a fixture in the Aberdeen line-up, playing in some unforgettable games. He was in the Dons team for the famous six-goal drubbing of Rangers in the semi final of the Scottish Cup on 10th April 1954, as well as the final itself, when Celtic won 2-1.

The following season, he never missed a game as Aberdeen lifted the League Championship for the first time, hitting the bar in the decisive single-goal victory at Clyde.

Prior to the start of the 1956-57 campaign, Jack was one of a party of seventeen Aberdeen players who went on a five week tour of North America. The trip did not get off to the best possible start, with the opening match against fellow tourists, Everton, postponed due to torrential rain. Jack, who had been out injured for a couple of months with a fractured elbow, then grabbed a treble in what became the opening game, an 8-0 stroll against the Montreal All-Stars.

Jack also hit a double in the rearranged match with Everton, a 3-3 draw, before coming off with a muscle injury.

For the next three seasons, Jack played in most of the Dons' matches, although by the time 1959-60 came around, his position on the wing had come under severe threat from George Mulhall.

His last appearance for Aberdeen was on the final Saturday of that season, a 2-0 Pittodrie win against Ayr United, by which time his achievements with the Dons included a League winner's medal, a League Cup winner's medal and participation in a trio of Scottish Cup Finals.

When he left Pittodrie, Jack returned to England to turn out for non-league Horden Colliery. It wasn't the last time the name Hather featured at Pittodrie, however, as Jack's son, John, was on the books in the seventies, making a couple of top-team appearances.

DAVID ROWSON

Legend of the future? Local lad David came through the Pittodrie ranks before making the breakthrough as a teenager. Injury problems have hampered the progress of the midfielder who has captained his country at under-21 level.

JIM HERMISTON

Full-back Jim joined the Dons from junior side, Bonnyrigg Rose in 1965 and for his first few seasons was understudy to first-choice right-back Jim Whyte. The Edinburgh-born youngster made his debut, along with central defender, Francis Munro, on 15th October 1966 in a 2-0 victory over Ayr United at Pittodrie.

It was during season 1969-70 that Jim finally established himself as a regular in the first team, making a number of appearances as a right half, notably in the famous cup-winning line-up of 11th April 1970, in the 3-1 win over Celtic.

Jim was almost a permanent fixture in Dons teams of the early seventies and for three seasons on the trot from 1971-72, he missed only a single league game each year. For the record, the games Jim sat out during that spell were a 2-0 win at home to Dunfermline Athletic on 2nd October 1971, a 1-1 draw at Arbroath on 14th April 1973 and the opening match of 1973-74, a scoreless draw at Motherwell on 1st September 1973.

In his latter days as an Aberdeen player, Jim skippered the side and in 1975 enjoyed the rare distinction of scoring from the spot in three successive games, at home to Dundee United (a 2-0 win on 29th March), away to Rangers (a 3-2 Ibrox defeat on 12th April) and at home again to Clyde (a 4-1 success on 19th April).

Towards the end of that season, Jim fell out with the club and announced his intention to retire from football. His last outing for the Dons was in a 3-1 success at Dunfermline Athletic, a game in which Dave Robb scored a hat-trick. Jim was also almost on target in that one but unfortunately at the wrong end–a downward header that missed Bobby Clark's post by inches!

To the surprise of most Aberdeen fans, 'Hermy' joined the local constabulary but after a relatively short spell in his new career, he emigrated to Australia, where he became one of the most respected players of the mid to late seventies 'Down Under'.

Although he never played for Scotland, Jim was on the fringe of international recognition on several occasions and was capped at Under-23 level.

STUART KENNEDY

ne of the original breed of overlapping full-backs, Stuart was signed by Aberdeen from Falkirk for a fee of £40,000 in the summer of 1976, making his debut in a 2-0 League Cup win over Kilmarnock on 14th August that summer.

Not exactly renowned as a goalscorer, he did manage a vital strike in his first season, the winner in a 2-1 victory at Rugby Park on 20th November 1976. By that juncture, Stuart had already picked up his first medal, having starred in the League Cup Final win over Celtic a fortnight previously.

Two seasons later, with the number two shirt now very much his own, Stewart grabbed three goals, all of them during the League Cup, which ended at the final stage. The strikes came in the 5-0, second round, first leg rout of Meadowbank Thistle on 30th August 1978, the 7-1, third round, second leg hammering of Hamilton Accies on 11th October and then in last four against Hibs on 13th December, when Stuart's extra time counter settled the outcome.

The following year, Stuart picked up a League Champions' medal, having played in all but one of the title-winning campaign. Interestingly, the one game he missed was the season's opener, when there was no indication of what was to come, as the Dons faltered 1-0 at Partick Thistle on 11th August 1979.

Stuart continued to give sterling service to club and also, by this time, country, having picked up the first of his eight caps. In 1981-82, the domestic collection was completed when Aberdeen won the Scottish Cup with the 4-1 extra time win against Rangers on 22nd May 1982.

The next season was looking even better. A Scottish Cup Final berth had already been secured, Stuart had scored his first goal in Europe in the 7-1 thumping of Sion of Switzerland in the preliminary round, first leg and unless a major disaster occurred, the European Cup Winners Cup Final was beckoning.

The Dons travelled to Belgium for their semi final second leg with Waterschei, 5-1 up from the Pittodrie game. In the event, the Belgian side reduced the deficit slightly, thanks to a single-goal win but for Stuart the game was a personal tragedy. He sustained a serious knee injury, which not only cruelly robbed him of the chance to play in a European final but more importantly, ended his career.

Stuart was a tremendous servant to Aberdeen Football Club, who, after being forced to retire returned to Falkirk to run his own public house.

GRAHAM LEGGAT

berdeen born and bred, Graham, one of the most talented stars ever to grace Pittodrie, joined the Dons from local side, Banks O'Dee, in the summer of 1953, playing in a red shirt for the first time on 12th September that year in a dismal single-goal league defeat at Stirling Albion.

Graham established himself as a first-team regular straight away and bagged nineteen goals in that first season. His haul included a strike in the famous 6-0 Scottish Cup semi-final thumping of Rangers on 10th April 1954 and he also picked up a runners-up medal in the competition, with the Dons going down 2-1 to Celtic.

A versatile forward, Graham played in all areas for the Dons, although he always looked at his best on the right wing. His eleven league goals helped the Dons to the title in 1954-55 and the following year he won the first of his eighteen Scottish caps. That season, 1955-56, was remarkable, too, as in his twenty-nine outings, Graham averaged a goal a game.

Nineteen fifty-six was also the year in which he fired the winning goal as the Dons defeated St Mirren in the final of the League Cup at Hampden on 22nd October.

The 1957-58 season was one which Graham would remember for a variety of reasons. He began in tremendous form and on 12th October 1957, scored an incredible five times in a 6-2 league victory at Airdrie.

Then, just a fortnight later, tragedy struck! In a Pittodrie clash with Partick Thistle, Graham ended up with a broken leg after coming off second best in a tackle with a Jags player and that was him out of action until February the following year.

He played his last Dons match on 26th April 1958, a match as disappointing as his first, being a 5-0 Ibrox drubbing by Rangers. In August, he was sold to Fulham for a bargain basement price of £16,000 and his talents were displayed at Craven Cottage for the next nine years, before he moved, firstly to Birmingham City and then Rotherham.

Following a spell with the backroom staff at Aston Villa, Graham emigrated to Canada, where he was involved in management before becoming one of the best-known faces in the country, as a top television sports presenter.

PAUL BERNARD

The Dons' first 'million pound player' when he was signed by Roy Aitken from Oldham Athletic in 1995. On his day, a class act although persistent injury absences have been a constant source of frustration to him. A good run displaying the kind of form he is certainly capable of would surely see him add to his current tally of two international caps.

TOMMY PEARSON

Tommy became the subject matter of football quiz nights all over the country by doing something that is unlikely to be repeated, namely playing for both Scotland and England!

The Lothian-born winger was transferred from Murrayfield Amateurs to Newcastle United in 1933 and during the Second World War was 'capped' by England, having been drafted in as an emergency player.

At the conclusion of the war, Tommy returned to St James' Park and was soon adding a dark blue jersey to his collection, when he was chosen to play for his 'real' country.

At the age of thirty-five, in February 1948, Tommy was signed by the Dons for a fee of £4000, making his debut in a 1-0 home defeat by Partick Thistle on Valentine's Day of that year. Despite that inauspicious start, his dazzling trickery on the wing soon made him a real crowd-puller, in particular his famous 'double shuffle'.

Despite the fact he was playing with the Dons during a particularly unsuccessful spell for the Pittodrie club, it says much for his ability that he still managed to attract his own band of fans in their thousands, who followed him everywhere, even in reserve matches.

With his fortieth birthday fast approaching, Tommy decided to call it a day on the playing front in 1953 and he turned out in Aberdeen colours for the last time at Tynecastle on 7th March. Sadly, his final outing as a Don was as successful as his first and the Pittodrie side were beaten 3-1. Tommy retired to pursue a career in sports journalism.

That was not the last Aberdeen was to see of Tommy and six years after leaving, he was back, this time as youth coach. In November 1959, he was appointed manager, in succession to Dave Shaw.

In a mirror image of when he was playing with the Dons, Tommy took over Aberdeen at not the best of times. The first half of the sixties saw the Dons never finish higher than sixth in the league table, whilst involvement in any of the cups rarely progressed past the initial stages. He stayed at Pittodrie until 1965, when, after a first round Scottish Cup exit at East Fife, he resigned, making way for the arrival of Eddie Turnbull.

Tommy then became a scout for former club, Newcastle United, before retiring home to Edinburgh, where sadly, he died in 1998.

MARK McGHEE

Born in Glasgow, the burly striker joined Bristol City as a youngster, before returning to Scotland with Morton in 1975, where his performances attracted the attentions of several sides, including Newcastle, who signed him at the tail end of 1977.

Mark never really settled at St James' Park and in March 1979, he was snapped up by the Dons for a fee of £80,000, almost half what Newcastle had paid for him.

His first match, ironically, was against former club, Morton, on 4th April 1979 and although it was a winning one, Neil Cooper bagging the only goal, Mark did miss a couple of real 'sitters'.

In fact, it took the strong-running Mark a while to settle with the Dons but when he did, he showed just what a valuable asset he was. In his first full season, he picked up a League Champions' medal, having participated in twenty-seven of the thirty-six matches.

The following year saw Mark being the only ever-present in the Aberdeen side in the league, with the Dons finishing in the runners-up position, seven points behind Celtic.

In the Scottish Cup Final on 22nd May 1982, by his own admission, Mark did not have his most impressive of matches. However, he still did sufficient to set the Dons on their way to victory with an extra-time header past Jim Stewart to make it 2-1, the game ending 4-1.

Like everyone else who was involved, 1982-83 was the real highlight of Mark's time at Pittodrie and it was, of course, his cross which was met by John Hewitt's head for the dramatic European Cup Winners' Cup winner.

The following year, Mark's last with Aberdeen, was another term of success after success. When he helped the Dons defeat Hamburg to lift the Super Cup, little was he to know he was playing against his next employers. A second League Champions' medal was added to the growing collection, before Mark put on a Dons shirt for the final time, the last stage of the Scottish Cup, with Celtic the opponents on 19th May 1984.

Fittingly, it was Mark who scored the winner, an extra-time strike to give the Dons a 2-1 victory, before moving to Hamburg for £285,000. He remained in Germany for a year-and-a-half before coming back to Scotland with Celtic.

Once he retired from the playing side of things, Mark moved into management and at time of writing, was awaiting his next appointment after being shown the door at Wolves.

SCOTT BOOTH

His partnership with Eoin Jess never quite fulfilled its undoubted potential, either at club or national level, and the classy striker moved under freedom of contract in the summer of 1997 to German giants Borussia Dortmund.

JOE MILLER

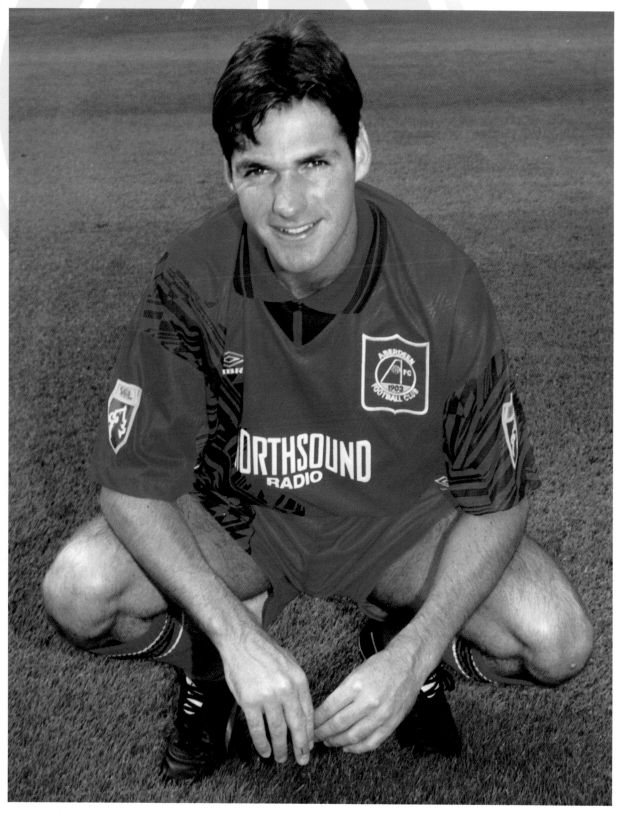

At his best as an old fashioned right-winger, Joe enjoyed two spells at Pittodrie, starring for Celtic in between and then moving to Dundee United in the summer of 1998. Left Tannadice a year later for Raith Rovers.

TEDDY SCOTT

Has been at Pittodrie since 1954, in a variety of positions, and was awarded a richly deserved testimonial in 1997, the highlight of which was the visit of Manchester United in January 1998. The esteem Teddy is held in is epitomised by the fact that Sir Alex Ferguson had changed the original date of the match as he did not want to insult the Pittodrie kit manager by bringing up an under-strength side.

DICK DONALD

Originally a player with Aberdeen in the twenties, Dick made a huge contribution to the development of Aberdeen Football Club as a director and then chairman, with the Richard Donald Stand, opened in 1993, named in his honour. After a long period of illness, Dick passed away on New Year's Eve 1994.

LEE RICHARDSON

A real fan's player, 'Rico' became an instant hit when he moved to the Dons from Blackburn Rovers in 1992. However, the battling midfielder did not always curry favour with the referees and he demanded a transfer after two seasons at Pittodrie, citing being unfairly treated by officials as the main reason for wanting to move. He was bought by Oldham.

NEIL SIMPSON

Simmie' was one of the most popular members of the Dons team of the 1980s and his commitment to the cause was greatly appreciated by the Red Army.

Neil came to Pittodrie on a 'S' form and made an early breakthrough into the first team in 1980, due to injuries to John McMaster and Gordon Strachan, making an instant impression in the heart of the Aberdeen midfield.

A tireless worker, Neil possessed boundless energy and international recognition came in 1983 as, of course, did the Scottish Cup and the European Cup Winners' Cup. However, the Bayern Munich game is remembered as Pittodrie's finest hour and Neil more than played his part in that game, scoring the equaliser at a packed Pittodrie to get the Dons back in the game.

Neil always seemed to weigh in with important goals including the opener in the 2-0 victory over Hamburg in the Super Cup at Pittodrie in 1984. A magnificent, sixty-yard run by Peter Weir ended with him reacting quickest to lash the ball home from the edge of the box. A history-making goal, it brought the Super Cup to Pittodrie, home of the only Scottish club to win two European trophies.

Neil's career went from strength to strength and coincided with Aberdeen's purple patch, as the club secured one trophy after another. Alex Ferguson's departure to Manchester United was the catalyst for several players leaving for pastures new but Simmie was a loyal servant and determined to play his part in the future of the club.

That determination proved to be his downfall. In October 1988, Rangers were at Pittodrie for a vital league match for both clubs. The Ibrox side were on the way back, thanks to David Murray's millions and the influence of Graeme Souness and this match, in particular, had a distinct edge to it. A tense, fraught encounter saw Neil commit a bad foul on Ian Durrant. The Rangers player was stretchered off the field and missed two-and-a-half years of his career. Simpson, totally unfairly in the eyes of Aberdeen fans, became public enemy number one.

If the truth be told, Neil Simpson's career ended that day, too. A media witch-hunt ensued and before the dust had settled, Durrant revealed he intended to sue Aberdeen and Neil for the events of that fateful day. Before long, he left Pittodrie and joined Newcastle United, before returning to Scotland with Motherwell and then, for a short spell, Cove Rangers. He retired in the early nineties and is currently SFA Development Officer for Moray.

PETER WEIR

The final member of the Gothenburg team to feature, Peter Weir will forever be remembered by Dons fans for his run that played such a crucial part in the goal by John Hewitt that won the European Cup Winners' Cup for the Dons in 1983.

In May 1981, Alex Ferguson was so determined to bring Peter to Pittodrie that he offered St. Mirren £200,000 plus Ian Scanlon in exchange for the services of the livewire left winger. The offer was too good for the Buddies to turn down and the deal went ahead.

Already a Scottish international, Peter made a quiet start to his Dons career but the UEFA Cup tie against Ipswich at Pittodrie witnessed him burst onto the scene and into the hearts of the Dons support.

With the game tied at 1-1, Peter went on a mazy run and left Town's outspoken English international full-back, Mick Mills, for dead, before lashing the ball past Paul Cooper. The cup holders were stunned but Peter wasn't finished yet and soon afterwards, set off on another magical run past Mills and finished the game off with a cool finish from the edge of the penalty area.

That game seemed to signal the start of Peter's Aberdeen career and he quickly showed the form that had alerted Fergie but less than two years later, he showed the whole of Europe that he was much more than your average Scottish player. A blistering performance in Gothenburg had left Real Madrid scratching their heads in disbelief at the quiet-spoken man from Johnstone.

A tall, pacy winger, Peter was a handful for any opposition defence and on his day, was one of the most devastating players in the Scottish game. His crossing ability was legendary and always seemed to find Eric Black, whose heading prowess was second-to-none. The Weir-Black combination had proved a profitable one for the Dons and was as good as a goal-a-game start on the opposition. Unsurprisingly, Aberdeen fans were more than disappointed when Black joined French outfit, Metz, in May 1986.

Peter's form also began to suffer, as he had become a marked man and the crunching challenges took their toll. In 1987, he joined Leicester City, although he almost returned to Pittodrie a year later, only for the English side to block the move. Nevertheless, he did return to Scotland with his first professional club, St Mirren, only to join Ayr United in 1990, before retiring from senior football in 1992.

PAUL MASON

Signed from Gronigen in 1988, the English born midfielder spent five good seasons with the Dons before being transferred to Ipswich Town, where he remained until retiring at the end of the 1998-99 campaign.

BILLY STARK

Former St Mirren man Billy never quite seemed to get the credit he deserved from some quarters of the Aberdeen support, although his contribution was certainly recognised by his team-mates. Made the step up to management at the conclusion of his playing days and is now in charge at Morton.

DOUG ROUGVIE

A native of Fife, Doug was signed by Aberdeen in 1972 from junior outfit, Dunfermline United. In his early time at Pittodrie, he was farmed out to now defunct junior side, Rosemount, before being recalled.

Although he notched up his opening first-team outing in a 1-0 League Cup reversal at Celtic on 9th August 1976, by the conclusion of season 1977-78, Doug had only made fourteen top team appearances, seven of which had been as a substitute.

In 1979, he was given an extended run in the first team at centre-half by Alex Ferguson but by the turn of the decade, the form of the Miller-McLeish partnership meant that big Doug spent most of the time playing at left-back.

He picked up a League winner's medal after playing twenty-five times as the Dons stormed to the title in 1979-80 and was very much an integral part of the Aberdeen successes of the early eighties.

A Scottish Cup winner's medal followed in 1981-82, with Doug playing at left-back in the final win over Rangers on 22nd May 1982 and then, twelve months later, the uncompromising defender was at right-back for the greatest night in the history of the club.

The switch had been caused by Stuart Kennedy's nasty injury, picked up in the European Cup Winners' Cup semi final, second leg clash in Belgium against Waterschei. The versatile John McMaster moved back to number three (it was nice and simple in those pre-squad number days!) with Doug switching to the right.

With the Cup Winners' Cup safely in the bag, Doug retained the right-back position for the Scottish Cup Final success against Rangers ten days later. In December, he played in the first leg of the European Super Cup success against Hamburg and a third Scottish Cup 'gong' was added to the collection on 19th May 1984, in the 2-1 win over Celtic at Hampden.

Somewhat surprisingly, the big defender decided to leave Pittodrie in the summer of 1984, joining Chelsea, before moving to Brighton, Shrewsbury, Fulham, Dunfermline and then Montrose, as player-manager. Spells as a Highland League manager followed at Huntly and Cove Rangers, with Doug continuing to turn out as he approached his fortieth birthday.

In a long career, Doug was capped once for his country, against Northern Ireland in 1984.

GORDON STRACHAN

**A** pivotal member of the great Aberdeen team of the eighties, Gordon came from Dundee to Pittodrie in November 1977 as one half of a player exchange deal which saw Jim Shirra move to Dens Park. A hard-working midfielder with boundless energy, Gordon had a knack of threading a ball through a crowded midfield and posed a big scoring threat.

His debut came in a 1-0 win at Tannadice over Dundee United on 5th November 1977 and indeed, Gordon took a while to settle at Pittodrie. Season 1979-80 saw the ginger haired midfielder burst onto the scene for the Dons and he enjoyed a fantastic campaign, which culminated in only the second Aberdeen League Championship in the club's history and Gordon nominated Scottish Player of the Year by his fellow professionals.

A stomach injury threatened his career in 1981 but luckily, he battled back and by the end of the year, he was running opposition defenders ragged for manager Alex Ferguson once again. As well as being a key member of the Aberdeen midfield, the player was now a vital part of the international set-up, having made his debut against Northern Ireland in 1980.

Gordon represented Scotland in two World Cups, his own personal highlight, a memorable celebration with the advertising boards following his strike against West Germany in Mexico '86. He retired from international football in 1992, having earned his fiftieth and final cap against Finland.

A constant joker on and off the field, Gordon was an expert at winding up his opponents and their support, a feat which endeared the 'wee man' all the more to the Dons support.

Pittodrie was stunned in May 1984, when he left the Club to join his former boss, Alex Ferguson, at Manchester United, where he enjoyed tremendous success. In 1985, he helped United win the FA Cup, before joining Leeds in 1989.

He skippered the Leeds side which gained promotion to the First Division in 1990 and then two years later, at the age of 35, he led the Elland Road side to the First Division Championship, the last to be contested before the introduction of the Premiership. In 1992, he made history when he was voted English Player of the Year, thus becoming the only player to win such an honour both north and south of the border.

In March 1995 he joined Ron Atkinson at Coventry City as assistant manager and succeeded Big Ron a year later. At present, he is the second-longest-serving manager in the Sky Blues' history, behind John Sillett.

MARK McGHEE & JOHN HEWITT

MILLER LEADS FROM THE FRONT

JENS PETERSEN

Signed from Danish side, Esbjerg, in January 1965, Jens was one of the last signings made by Tommy Pearson. He made his debut, along with fellow Danes, Jorgen Ravn and Lief Mortensen, in a 3-1 win against Third Lanark on the 27th of that month.

That match gave Jens and his fellow countrymen a gentle baptism to Scottish football but they were brought straight back down to earth three days later, when they were absolutely hammered, 8-0, by Celtic at Parkhead. In his early days at the club, Jens struggled somewhat and he had only made four top-team appearances by the end of that season.

Jens was nothing if not a battler and he worked away in the reserves, being restored to the first team at the end of October 1965, from whence he became the regular first choice sweeper.

In the following season, Aberdeen reached the last four of the League Cup, where they lost to Rangers after a replay. In the Scottish Cup, they went one better, ending as runners-up to Celtic, being beaten by a Willie Wallace brace at Hampden on 29th April 1967.

Later that same year, on 6th September, Jens took part and scored in the Dons' first-ever competitive (although, not in this case!) European match, the 10-0 Pittodrie thumping of Icelandic amateurs, K.R. Kevlavik. Aberdeen cruised through 14-1 on aggregate, only to be brought back down to earth by Standard Liege of Belgium in the next round.

Jens became the Pittodrie club captain in 1968 and in season 1968-69, he played in all fifty of Aberdeen's matches, thirty-four in the league, six each in the League and Scottish Cups and four in the Fairs Cup.

The popular Dane stayed with the Dons for another full season, although he had faded out of the first team picture by the time the Cup Final, won this time round by Aberdeen, was staged. He made his last appearance for Aberdeen on 9th March 1970 in the 2-0 home defeat by Hibs.

Of the three Danes who made their Dons debuts on the same day, Jens was by far the most successful. In 1999, he made a nostalgic trip back to Pittodrie, all the way from Copenhagen, for a tribute evening for the manager who was boss for most of his time at Pittodrie, Eddie Turnbull.

The Danish connection lives on at Pittodrie with the appointment in the summer of 1999 of the new Aberdeen management team of Ebbe Skovdahl and Tommy Moller-Nielsen. Back in Denmark, Jens will undoubtedly be keeping a close eye on how they fare at his former club.

DAVE SHAW

Dave's first senior club was Hibs, who he joined from Grange Rovers just prior to the outbreak of the Second World War. On the cessation of hostilities, he resumed his career at Easter Road, turning in such excellent performances that he was rewarded with an international call-up.

When he skippered Hibs in the 1946-47 Scottish Cup Final, a game won by the Dons, 2-1, little was he to know that the opposition that day would be his second and only other professional club.

Dave signed for the Dons in the summer of 1950 and was immediately installed as club captain, making his debut on the opening Saturday of the new season on 12th August. Also playing for Aberdeen that day for the first time was Alan Boyd, a close-season capture from Queen's Park and both contributed to an exciting, high-scoring 4-3 League Cup win over Clyde.

He spent three seasons as a player with Aberdeen, his final outing being the 1-0 defeat by Rangers in the Scottish Cup Final replay on 29th April 1953, after which he took up the post of trainer at Pittodrie. This was not an entirely new role for Dave, as he had been performing the dual positions of player and trainer since the departure of Jock Pattillo earlier in the year.

Dave spent a couple of seasons as trainer and certainly his influence was there for all to see, as Aberdeen lifted the League Championship for the first time in their history in season 1954-55.

In the summer of 1955, following the departure of boss, Dave Halliday, to Leicester City, Dave was offered the manager's position at Aberdeen Football Club and in his first season in charge, he guided the team to League Cup glory.

Unfortunately, that was to be that in terms of success for Dave, although, to be fair, injuries to key players such as Alec Young, Paddy Buckley and Archie Glen certainly did not help.

In November 1959, Dave decided to call it a day in the hotseat and gratefully returned to what he best enjoyed, namely being a trainer. He remained at Pittodrie until retiring in 1967 and died in 1977.

WILLIE YOUNG

A relative unknown when he joined Aberdeen Football Club from Seton Athletic in 1969, Willie had an immediate impact on the first team, making his debut, aged just 18, against Dundee in a 2-1 win on 18th September 1970.

By 1971, he was a regular in the first team at Pittodrie, where he had formed an impressive central defensive partnership with Martin Buchan. The 1971-72 season also saw the giant centre-half notch his first senior goal for the Dons, netting the winner in a grudge match against Hibernian, who were by then managed by the man who gave him his debut at Pittodrie, Eddie Turnbull.

Having opened his scoring account for the Pittodrie side, Willie grew in confidence and coped admirably when he lost his partner at the heart of the defence, following Martin Buchan's move to Manchester United.

A controversial figure, his international career was curtailed at Under-23 level, following an alleged incident in a public house in Copenhagen. Five players were reportedly involved in a dispute over a bill and were thrown out of a nightclub by the Danish Police. Billy Bremner was also reputedly felled in the team's hotel later in the evening but the end result was that Willie was banned from International football, along with club team-mate, Arthur Graham and Joe Harper (Hibs), Bremner (Leeds) and Pat McCluskey (Celtic).

Although the ban was subsequently lifted in 1977, Willie would never play for his country again. Meanwhile, his club form had continued to improve and in 1973, the red haired defender was made club captain by Jimmy Bonthrone.

In a disappointing period for everyone connected with Pittodrie, Willie was a shining light and his impressive form saw the player go from strength to strength. However, just as the alleged Copenhagen incident ended his international career, the events of the Dundee United game at Pittodrie in September 1975 proved to be Willie's final appearance in the red of Aberdeen.

The Dons were trailing 1-0 heading into the second half, when Joe Smith received his marching orders following a scuffle with Paul Hegarty. Bonthrone withdrew his number five in a tactical switch, with striker Billy Pirie taking the stopper's place. A heated argument ensued between Willie and his manager, ending with the player throwing his shirt at the Dons boss and storming down the tunnel.

Within a week, Willie had joined Tottenham Hotspur for £100,000 and he had further spells with Arsenal, Nottingham Forest and Norwich City, before ending his career with Brighton.

GARY SMITH

Former Falkirk defender Gary has enjoyed plenty of ups and downs in his two spells with the Pittodrie side.
In between, Gary spent a season trying his luck in Europe with French outfit Rennes.

ALEX FERGUSON

Dons fans can be rightly proud that the man who went on to become, arguably, the most successful club manager ever, learned many of his tricks of the trade with the Dons. Rightly awarded the Freedom of the Granite City in 1999, Sir Alex still retains extremely close links with his former club.